Advance Praise for *Learning Leadership through Loss*

I have always felt that the greatest lessons come to us through pain and hardship. This book is a must-read for every person in business—especially women who face a variety of seemingly insurmountable situations during the course of their lives.

—Amma Johnson
Singer, songwriter, entrepreneur

Learning Leadership through Loss is definitely NOT the typical book on the topic of leadership. Sylvia's compelling story of her own dramatic personal loss challenges you to examine your life losses and their impact on your leadership style, growth, and development.

—Crystal L. Weand
Director, Division of Workforce Development & Training
Pennsylvania Department of Health
Harrisburg, PA

This awesome book is the answer to moving beyond loss of any type. Sylvia poignantly reminds readers that leadership is not just about the goals we have achieved but about the struggles we have overcome.

—Patricia A. Bucek
Vice President of Chamber Operations
Harrisburg Regional Chamber & CREC

In this very personal book Sylvia shows us how we can be authentic and visionary leaders by changing our view of life's most daunting obstacles. Using her own story of loss and subsequent growth and development, she provides clear guidance about how to become a strong leader because of what you've lost.

—Rev. Sharron R. Blezard
Assistant to the Bishop
Lower Susquehanna Synod, PA (ELCA)

A rare jewel in the world of leadership, this magnificent book is irrefutably a profound and compelling read that teaches both seasoned and emerging leaders how to positively use loss to develop exceptional skills. Practical, provocative, and engaging to the end, this book is a true winner!

—Kim Kreider Umble
President and CEO
Lebanon Family Health Services

Although *Learning Leadership through Loss* by Sylvia Hepler pulls on your heartstrings, it also gives you strength, wisdom, and courage to move forward in your leadership journey, regardless of industry or arena.

—Joylyn Conklin
Director of Client Services
KNOVEX, LLC

As a result of reading *Learning Leadership through Loss*, which is filled with riveting and insightful personal accountings, readers will be inspired and motivated to make significant life changes and overcome both large and small work-related problems by implementing some fresh strategies.

—Karen Snider
President, Susquehanna Consulting
Harrisburg, PA

Although Sylvia's loss is not unique, her story about how she dealt with it is. She viewed loss as an opportunity to build leadership skills—a real paradigm shift. Her strategies for leveraging personal pain work. This book educates leaders while reading like a novel.

—Asha Makam
Business development consultant
Mechanicsburg, PA

Sylvia Hepler's new book, *Learning Leadership through Loss,* inspired me to refocus on why I do what I do—and how I do it. I think I lost a bit of my professional and career vision along the way, and this book helped me get back in touch with it.

—Aviv S. Bliwas, Esquire
Law Offices of Aviv Bliwas, Camp Hill, PA

Sylvia created a masterpiece that moves you to tears, kicks you in the gut, and leaves you wanting to turn the pages fast. A beautifully written, transparent journal of hope, this book has the power to serve others who aspire to up their leadership game.

—A. Drayton Boylston
Founder, The Executive Coaching University, LLC

LEARNING LEADERSHIP through LOSS

SYLVIA D. HEPLER

*L*EARNING
LEADERSHIP
THROUGH *L*OSS

This publication is designed to provide accurate and authoritative information in regard to the subject matter covered. It is sold with the understanding that the author is not engaged in rendering professional services. If legal, accounting, medical, psychological, or any other expert assistance is required, the services of a competent professional person should be sought.

Library of Congress Control Number: 2015931239

ISBN: 978-1-934509-82-1
Printed in the United States of America

Editing by Gwen Hoffnagle
Cover design by 2FacedDesign.com

Dedication

To leaders everywhere who have lost someone or something important in this life and wonder how they can use that experience to serve both individuals and organizations differently and wisely. Where do you see yourself?

job terminations
illnesses or unwanted health conditions
physical disabilities
marital strife
financial loss
physical, emotional, sexual, or financial abuse
separation or divorce
death
substance abuse
aging
alterations in physical appearance
infirmities
deteriorating elderly parents
mental health challenges
geographical moves
new jobs
unemployment
empty nest syndrome
loss of friendships
loss of reputation
loss of respect

loss of living space through fire or flood
loss of support for significant life choices you've made

To Don Moyer who asked me to tell this story someday in a way that would benefit and inspire others.

To Frank Bach who unfailingly and lovingly cared for me during one of the most painful periods of my life.

Acknowledgments

I am grateful to Sheldon Vanauken, award-winning author and long-ago mentor and friend, for believing that I could write a book years before I believed it.

I am also grateful to Joan L. Nichols, former high school English teacher and friend, who, with a critical eye, eagerly read all of my magazine articles published between 1987 and 1992 with sincere appreciation. I am sorry she is no longer alive to read this book.

I thank all of my previous and current clients (whose names have been changed to protect their identity and confidentiality) whose stories, in overview form, appear in Part II of *Learning Leadership through Loss*. It has been a great privilege and honor to facilitate your desired, necessary transformations and to learn from you during the process.

Contents

PART I

My Story

PART II

Positioned to Lead

Introduction

At some time or other every human being experiences loss. For women, it seems to be woven into the fabric of our lives from birth to death. Decades of observation have shown me that most women experience a greater variety of losses than men—and feel them more intensely. There are exceptions.

In my teens and twenties I didn't understand the long-term positive power of loss—that ultimately it can position us to do great things. Back then I didn't realize that by itself, loss has no value, and that we give it significance only through what we do with it. Instead I laser-focused on the person or opportunity I'd lost and the associated painful impact, never considering that what I'd learned would allow me to assign some deeper meaning to it. I only grasped a fraction of what I needed to see.

This book is about loss and its connection to leadership. I didn't think about such a linkage when I was young. Reflecting on my childhood and youth, I remember with certainty that neither loss nor leadership were discussed openly in the house in which I grew up. Today I am aware that my parents, working professionals and community volunteers, were recognized as leaders in their respective fields. I am also aware that both of them had known loss before and after their four children were born. I am sorry they chose not to talk about how their losses molded them as individuals and developed them as leaders. Had they done this, negotiating my own labyrinth of trying to discern the relationship between loss and leadership might not have taken so long.

When I was seven my parents started to argue for reasons my siblings and I only partially understood. This new, loud phenomenon in the evenings and on weekends left me trembling and afraid. It also introduced me to the concept of loss. Those vicious verbal battles took away my sense of security at home. They also stripped me of childhood innocence.

My maternal grandmother's sudden death when I was thirteen illustrated the stark finiteness and evolution of life. My mother, immersed in inconsolable grief, never fully recovered. Her mouth smiled, but her eyes often fixed on us with an empty stare. She became more introverted and quiet. She rarely laughed. With sadness and random anger we children noticed a different person—the familiar one previously known to us was gone.

A decade later my mother suffered a heart attack after seeing doctors for years without a specific diagnosis. Despite the fact that my nursing-student sister and I dragged her to the car by ourselves and drove too slowly to the nearest emergency room, she survived the event. However, on the day she was scheduled for release from the hospital, she underwent a cardiac catheterization to determine the extent of artery damage. The procedure killed her. Something went terribly wrong. My father was informed that her death, a total shock to the medical personnel, was horrific. Upon receiving the news all of us felt numb. On that awful October day we didn't know that our lives had changed forever. I was just twenty-three, out on my own, and engrossed in my first teaching job. My youngest sister was a freshman in high school.

I stood at a crossroads then. Circumstances seemed to indicate that I should give up my independent living arrangement to help my father, a shell of himself and barely functioning, finish raising my youngest sister and handle daily chores. Because I'd been away from home for only a short time, I preferred not to do that. Yet I thought my presence might provide some much-needed stability and guidance for a grieving, floundering teenager. On a conscious level I didn't think about assuming a leadership role the day I packed my belongings and returned home. I just thought about doing the right thing.

None of this was easy. In his grief my dad proved to be more difficult than usual, and my fifteen-year-old sister resented my attempts to set boundaries around her social life. She rebelled, and we bickered. It was a stressful time for the three of us. But the premature loss of my mother and my decision to move back home taught me a lot about survival, resilience, and leadership. Or so I thought. Although thirty-seven years ago I certainly didn't welcome what I now regard as an initial, basic course in grief recovery, I made mental note of each lesson as it unfolded over thirteen months until my sister went to live with her godmother in the Midwest. A large part of me believed that this education, taxing but essential, would come in handy down the road. Of course I didn't know when, where, or how.

The answers to those private, silent questions came rapidly after I married my first husband, Don. It's not surprising that more lessons presented themselves before and after his death, and those already occupying a notch on my belt advanced to the next level. I was acutely aware that a steady series of small and large losses was changing me. I sensed I'd never be the same person, and most days that was okay. I didn't resist. I accepted it instinctively without understanding the details. With benign curiosity I saw myself as a mound of clay spinning on a potter's wheel, open to a new *me*.

In the months following Don's death I began to think about what my dramatic loss—or any loss—could mean to me and others both within the current bigger picture and long term. After all that I'd suffered I *needed* it to mean something beyond the sheer fact of it. I didn't want to forget what happened or its impact; I wanted to *do* something with it. I needed to make it count. Throughout the ages many people who have borne traumatic growth have felt this way. I certainly wasn't unique. However, I was eager to begin using what I'd learned, and the first opportunity couldn't come soon enough. The transformed Sylvia, now refined, possessed rich knowledge, insights, and ideas to share. Not only was I stronger, but also more complete, more confident, and more attuned to life. I felt inspired to leave my stamp on everything I touched.

If you're in a leadership role at work or in your community, know that I wrote this book for you. If you aspire to lead people and projects someday down the road, trust that my story and message are for you, too. I want you to understand that our life losses can be teachers, and that if we allow it, they can transform us into profoundly competent people who function at an unexpectedly high level—people ready to lead and to serve. While our losses, regardless of intensity or type, affect each of us emotionally, psychologically, spiritually, and even physically, they need not cripple us. Instead they open the door to possibility. I've seen it firsthand.

The first thing I suggest you do—before you turn the page and start to read Part I—is to take a few deep breaths and identify the various losses you've experienced since childhood. Maybe you're going through some sort of loss right now. Be honest with yourself. Don't pretend or play the game of denial. Once you have this clarity, think about how these losses have influenced your life choices, career trajectory, and work performance. Consider how you might have used them as handy excuses for holding back, hiding out, staying safe, or playing small. Take a few moments to reflect on how your losses—even those that go back twenty years—make you feel today. Even if you believe they don't have an effect on your feelings, residue matters. This contemplation is important for everybody, but especially leaders, because your feelings drive your decisions, direct your actions, determine your approach, and shape your style. Others are impacted—scores, hundreds, thousands. Make no mistake; your losses affect what you do, how you do it, and why.

At this point in my life I intuitively know—and appreciate—that leadership emerges from our circumstances, particularly the ones we label "bad." That's not guaranteed, but it is possible. I know because it happened to me. In *Learning Leadership through Loss*, a sincere and deliberate labor of love, you will read my story of loss and how I transcended it and triumphed. Within these pages lies an abridged yet raw accounting of how I was chipped and carved by the chisel of loss and how I eventually leveraged a very dramatic loss to lead. To be candid, over the last few years I've wondered if I'd have bothered to embrace the leadership positions I've held had I not endured it. Of course I cannot know that answer with certainty. If I had chosen the path of leadership without having known the loss, I might have been a good leader. However, I believe I've been a *better* leader over thirty-odd years because of it.

I chose not to waste my loss. I ask you not to waste yours.

To download my free assessment entitled "How Is Your Loss Keeping You Stuck?" simply go to www.launchinglives.biz/pdfs/Book assessment.pdf.

PART I

My Story

Chapter 1

PREPARING FOR THE WORST

In the spring of 1979 I married a person with juvenile diabetes who was going blind. I was twenty-five and he was thirty-six. During several prenuptial conversations with an ophthalmologist at Hershey Medical Center in Pennsylvania, I learned the prognosis wasn't good. Total blindness—the worst possible outcome—could happen. We left each appointment feeling uneasy.

Twenty-seven years of diabetes had taken a toll on Don's body. By the time we discussed marriage he had received a diagnosis of retinopathy, a serious retina-damaging condition that afflicts 80 percent of people who have had diabetes long term. It was irreversible.

Looking back, I realize that I thought I understood the challenges we might have to face in our life together. Today? I conclude that my understanding was based on one doctor's medical knowledge and experience. Period. Unlike English, the French language offers two different words for the verb *to know*. *Savoir* refers to knowing a fact; knowing a process; knowing a poem or a story by heart. *Connaitre*, on the other hand, refers to knowing a person and being very familiar with someone or something. I see now that my *knowing* three decades ago was merely the *savoir* version. The *connaitre* version, hard won, came later.

Part of me hesitated to marry a man whose health was slowly being destroyed by disease. Lying in bed at night I told myself that if I truly loved Don, none of this should matter. Unfortunately, it did matter. On one occasion I almost backed out. Later Don told me that while he would have been hurt if I'd have said no, he wouldn't have tried to change my mind. "I wouldn't have tried to talk you into marrying me precisely because I love you and I have some idea of what's in store," he told me.

At the time of our wedding Don had little to no functional vision in his left eye. Sight in that eye was limited to light perception—an annoying glare. Beginning in late 1977 he began to receive laser treatments to alleviate the hemorrhaging of blood vessels in both eyes. Successful burn treatments fused weak vessels of the retina together. This process typically slows down retinopathy progression. The treatments, twenty minutes in length, triggered some physical discomfort and were extremely expensive. While laser treatment gradually diminishes peripheral vision, having those treatments was better than not having them. He had to sacrifice some vision to preserve some vision. Quite simply, Don chose to continue the laser therapy to buy time. He didn't want to go blind completely, and he certainly didn't want to lose his job. Still, only so many burn treatments could be done.

By the fall of 1979 Don had serious difficulty driving at night. Months later he complained about this situation to his ophthalmologist who recommended a relatively new surgical procedure called a vitrectomy. The vitrectomy removed the vitreous fluid in Don's left eye so that blood leakage would not cloud his vision further. In a best-case scenario this surgery would have actually restored a little bit of sight, but to date there had been no notable successes. Of course Don told the doctor and me that somebody had to be first. Perhaps he'd be the one.

After a hospital stay of two-and-a-half days, Don returned home. We waited two weeks to obtain the results of the procedure. Don was required to stay calm and relatively still at home. Several times each day I administered special eye drops and salve, and changed his bandages. I cringed whenever I removed one bandage to replace it with another. Bloodshot didn't begin to describe the appearance of that eye. Occasionally I felt sick to my stomach, but I never mentioned this to Don. I didn't want him to think I couldn't do what had to be done, and I didn't want him to get upset over how I felt about it.

Finally the checkup visit with the doctor rolled around on the calendar. In great anticipation of at least a little positive news, I drove us
to the medical center. Don was quiet during the drive. He probably was
afraid to say what he hoped.

Unfortunately the outcome of the vitrectomy was poor. The opera-
tion did not restore any vision at all. Through sophisticated ophthal-
mology equipment Don's left eye looked exactly as it had prior to the
procedure. The emotional letdown was huge for both of us. It was significant for the physician, too. He kept apologizing over and over again
for the failed surgery that wasn't his fault. On the ride back home Don
and I remained lost in our own private thoughts. Although we didn't
talk, I had a strong sense that already he worried about the day when
he'd need to quit working. A salesman all of his life, he worked at that
time for a radio station that expected their account executives to be on
the road. No exceptions.

A few weeks after Don's recovery from surgery in March of 1980,
while driving to a job-related appointment, he hit a twelve-year-old boy
on a bicycle. He never saw the boy or the bike in the middle of the
city street. When he finally saw something moving in front of his car,
he swerved to avoid contact, but he didn't react quickly enough. He
smashed into the bicycle, and the child fell off. Luckily he'd only been
going about twenty-five miles per hour. Although both he and the boy
were shaken, no one was physically hurt. To our great relief, no lawsuit
followed this incident.

The next day the ophthalmologist performed a field-of-vision test
on Don's eyes. The results were stunning. He had twenty degrees of
vision, the official definition of legal blindness. A line had now been
crossed. There was no going back. A person cannot drive a vehicle with
this diagnosis without serious ramifications.

When Don informed his employer of his visual status and what it
meant, his sales manager advised him to keep on driving. The message was this: If something bad happens, it happens. Shocked by the
response, Don informed his boss that he refused to do that. It was too
risky. He suggested that the company consider hiring a driver for him
for a minimal financial investment, but neither the owner nor his manager showed interest in exploring that option. So Don resigned. As it

turned out, the radio station lost a sizable chunk of revenue over the next couple of years as a result of losing one of their highest-producing salesmen.

The only good thing in this devastating situation was the disability insurance checks Don received through his previous employer. This money was intended to supplement Social Security Disability (SSD) benefits. To our surprise Don was denied SSD not once but twice over twelve months. What a blow to our bank account! As an elementary remedial reading teacher I earned a meager salary. Going to Dairy Queen for an ice cream cone was a treat.

After the second denial Don's nerves were shot. He knew he had the right to contact an administrative law judge to review his case, and decided to exercise it. During that excruciating initial telephone conversation he was informed that he didn't meet the requirements for SSD. When he asked the assistant to tell him the criteria for legal blindness, she told him "twenty degrees of vision or less." His face red from anger and stress, he said to her, "Then what the hell are we arguing about?" Immediately his application went from pending to approved.

With that crisis behind us, we started to discuss Don's boredom. For a full year he had sat at home, virtually unoccupied, with no real purpose or direction. Occasionally he cleaned our apartment and did some laundry. To vary his routine he took a bus into nearby Lebanon for coffee or lunch in a casual restaurant once or twice a month. Much to my frustration, some days he never got out of his pajamas. On scores and scores of afternoons I came home from work and found him sitting in his recliner in the living room, a flat expression pasted on his face. I wanted to relay little anecdotes about the children at school, but he would just stare straight ahead, saying nothing. He showed no interest. He was bitter. His life revolved around grieving the loss of his driver's license and his career. For many years he'd enjoyed a busy work life interacting with colleagues and clients. Now he had nothing meaningful to do.

In the fall of 1980 Don realized that he needed more help dealing with his blindness than I could give him or he could give himself. Somewhere along the line he recognized that he required professional guidance, and perhaps even a bit of counseling. One afternoon Don surprised me when he told me that he'd contacted the National Federation for the Blind in Baltimore. He'd talked about this organization previously but hadn't taken any action. I stayed silent whenever he raised the subject, trusting that he'd call them when he was ready. For half an hour he recounted the details of the conversation he'd had with the woman at the NFB. He sounded interested, even a little enthused. Yet I sensed his hesitation about visiting their headquarters for a five-day workshop, despite the warm invitation extended.

It took three separate invitations before Don gave in and bought his bus ticket in December of 1980. I could not go with him, as that was against organizational procedure. Blind people were instructed to go alone. Of course this visit took place before the era of cell phones; thus I stayed in Lebanon and wondered what was happening over the scheduled five days.

When I picked him up at the bus station at the end of the week, Don wasted no time telling me about his experiences. He was animated. He smiled, something I didn't see him do very often anymore. He told me about the white cane lessons and being expected to walk around Baltimore with only his cane. What I always remember in detail, however, is the message he relayed from the president of the NFB, Dr. Kenneth Jernigan. As a newly blind woman cried openly during a group meeting, Dr. Jernigan told everyone in the room that despite what they thought, they had three choices: they could continue to gripe about their blindness for the rest of their lives, making everybody around them miserable; they could commit suicide, telling the world they'd given up; or they could accept their situation and do something with it. That stay in Baltimore was clearly a turning point for Don— and probably for the others in attendance, too. Rather quickly I noticed that we were about to enter a different phase of this chaos, and things would improve. The trip hadn't cost us anything except Don's time and a bus ticket.

Things changed as Don began to establish his identity as a blind man. I understood that he needed to do this, and that it wouldn't happen overnight. I gave him the freedom to do it his way. After everything we'd been through so far it was hard to be patient, but I took each day as it came. It wasn't long before Don discovered that there was a local chapter of the NFB in our area. Once he connected with those folks, doors opened. He met other blind people and gained lots of essential, practical information about how to live as a visually impaired individual. He shared this knowledge with me regularly, so we were both getting an education.

As a result of what we learned I developed a paper-clip system that allowed him to identify the various denominations of money in his wallet. I arranged his clothing in his closet a certain way so that he could identify the black pants from the brown ones. Making his daily existence less stressful was about keeping objects in the same place and devising simple systems. The established order gave him a sense of control and security.

One morning after I'd gone to work Don happened to listen to a radio talk show that captured his attention. The local hospital sought volunteers. This ad planted a seed in his mind, a seed that germinated and grew into an opportunity he'd never anticipated. What if he phoned the director of volunteers and talked to her about the possibility of joining her sizable team? He and I discussed it thoroughly. Within a week or so he made that call. And that conversation changed his world. At first the director, Diane, explained that she wasn't sure what someone with significant visual impairment could do at the hospital, but she promised to think about it. Don told me later that she seemed hesitant about encouraging him to move forward with the process. Curious about what would happen, he pressed her to mail him an application.

When it arrived we completed it together. Since Don couldn't read the questions, I read them to him and he formulated his responses. I wrote what he quoted in the designated spaces. Then, after careful review, we sent it off and waited to hear from Diane. She called within a few days and offered him a chair in her general office area. Accepting her offer to answer the phone and handle simple tasks, Don started "work" at the hospital in April of 1981. He now had a reason to get out of bed in the morning, and I noticed a big difference in his attitude.

At that time I was employed at the same hospital, working alongside twenty-five other women of various ages in the business office forty hours a week. I didn't apply for a job there because Don was stationed onsite, but partially because I knew the community hospital's benefits package exceeded that of any other employer in the area except for the Veterans Administration Hospital on the other side of town. Our situation demanded more health insurance security than I had at my accounts receivable job with the school district. To be candid, I disliked that job for several reasons. Once I learned how to do it, I found it repetitive and dull. Many of the women were mean, and my boss had no idea how to supervise people. Without exaggerating, it was a disaster. On most days I counted the hours until quitting time. Although it wasn't satisfying for me, the job provided a good paycheck and the benefits we needed.

When Don started his volunteer tenure, he got around by holding onto someone's arm. His vision had deteriorated to the point where he could no longer walk safely by himself. He'd ordered a white aluminum folding cane from an independent living aids catalog that featured products for blind people, but it sat on a closet shelf at home. He rarely mentioned it. I finally figured out that talking about that cane made his visual deficiency too real. He wasn't ready to use it.

A few accidents within a week changed his mind. One Sunday he fell up and down the church steps, ripping the knee of his suit pants. In a small grocery store he walked into a support beam, smacking his forehead hard against steel. The last straw occurred when he bumped his shin into a wooden delivery cart with sharp edges in the hospital basement, bleeding into his shoes. These incidences showed Don that using his cane had become a necessity, so with regular practice he learned how to use it correctly.

The first time Don decided to use his cane in public we went to dinner at a hotel out of town. It was a Friday night, and the restaurant was full. As we walked slowly across the room to our table, I saw people staring at us, their forks raised in mid-air. Conversations stopped. My heart pounded. I wanted to run away. I wanted to be anywhere but there. Although I chose not to share my feelings with Don, I didn't relax during the meal. Every time I looked up I noticed fellow diners stretching their necks to catch a glimpse of the blind man eating his steak. That evening's experience initiated me to celebrity life. I didn't want to be that kind of a celebrity. I hated people looking at us. I hated people looking at me and wondering what I was doing with someone like Don. Although I never grew completely comfortable providing folks with a show, I managed to adjust.

Over a period of a few months Don became adept at walking alone with the cane. This constant companion enabled him to feel safe as he increased his personal mobility. It helped him locate stairs and curbs, protected him from protruding objects, and warned him of immediate dangers such as soda cans parked in the middle of a pavement. Further, the cane alerted drivers and pedestrians to the fact that he was visually compromised. Eventually we celebrated his first navigation of one city block from the front door of the hospital building where he worked to the building where I worked. This involved crossing a busy and some-times noisy side street. It was no small victory.

At home I'd been cutting his meat before serving his meal. I arranged the food strategically so he could find it. We pretended the plate was a clock: I placed his potatoes at twelve o'clock, the green veg-etable at three o'clock, a piece of protein at six o'clock, and a slice of tomato at nine o'clock. Applesauce or coleslaw went into a side dish positioned above his fork in the place setting. The water glass went above his knife, even though Don rarely used one anymore. By doing things this way he was able to enjoy his meals more than if he had to struggle to locate the various types of food. It also eliminated the need to push food around with his fingers. When we ate in restaurants, I usually took his plate from the server once it arrived at the table and rearranged the items in the familiar fashion before setting it in front of Don. It was important to him that he not be embarrassed in public. Eating like a child or a person lacking manners was not something he was willing to do.

To our relief, that summer our lives fell naturally into a reasonable routine. We went to work, watched movies, and talked for hours out on the porch. That peace, welcome as it was, didn't last. Early one weekday morning in October while in the bathroom combing my hair, I heard a strange cry from our bedroom. Deeply concerned, I raced across the hall. There I found Don trying to prop himself up in the bed, tears streaming down his cheeks. Struggling to form the words, he told me the other shoe had dropped during the night. All of his vision was gone. His world had been reduced to a thick, gray fog, forcing him to join the ranks of the totally blind, representing 10 percent of all those statistically designated as blind. My heart sank.

Chapter 2

SETTING AN EXAMPLE

The final quarter of 1981 was rough. Don fell into a deep depression again, almost to the extent of the pit he had experienced after resigning from his job. Total blindness, we found, was worse than we'd imagined. To his horror Don discovered that he had no light perception in either eye, and absolutely no ability to see shapes or movements directly in front of him. He described it to me as walking around in the ocean at night. The emotional implications were huge. Both of us were crying inside. Although neither of us talked about it, we knew the divorce rate was 75 percent for visually discordant couples.

During the last few weeks of that year Don realized he had to do something to motivate himself to keep on living. While he and I regularly attended a support group in a neighboring county, he'd learned that no such group exclusively for blind persons existed in our area. That knowledge got him thinking. Why couldn't *he* start a group? The downside was that he didn't know anyone else who was legally or totally blind. However, he did know an organization that kept a list of names: The Lebanon Lions Club.

Upon contacting the Lions Club, he was told that previous attempts to launch a support group for the blind had failed. But Don was persistent, and he obtained names and phone numbers through the club's nurse. By January of 1982 he was making calls to everybody on that list. Quite a few folks expressed interest in becoming involved if such a group got off the ground. The hospital graciously consented to let the group gather in one of their first-floor classrooms, and the Lions Club generously made a commitment to transport members to all monthly meetings. Don was grateful.

The initial meeting took place in March. When forty people showed up, we cheered. By the end of that evening the group had chosen a name, and INSIGHT was born. INSIGHT had been Don's recommendation. Over the next couple of meetings the attendees determined that it existed for a three-fold purpose: to support each other and their families in coping with blindness; to educate the public about blindness; and to obtain relevant information from all federal, state, and local agencies that dealt with visually impaired individuals. During meetings, members shared experiences and discussed practical matters that focused primarily on housing, benefits, transportation, and jobs. Public image and self-image entered these conversations, too. In time the group developed a brochure as well as a comprehensive list of resources.

From INSIGHT's inception Don insisted it should be an organization of blind people run by blind people. He didn't want it to be just another entity managed by sighted folks. He believed the blind needed to learn how to do their own work, make their own decisions, pay their own bills, and carry their own weight. He felt strongly about preparing them to become more independent and less dependent. Thus he rejected handouts for himself and the group. He said blind people needed to prove their desire to overcome the second-class economic and social status they claimed they hated. While most members agreed, a small number opposed this view. A line was drawn in the sand.

Not only did I drive Don to INSIGHT meetings for several years, but I stayed for most of them. I got to know the members, and I appreciated the opportunity to expand my education about what it's like to be blind. As support group facilitator, Don invited various guest experts to provide programs that helped people improve the quality of their daily lives. Featured presenters included representatives from the Pennsylvania Bureau of Blindness and Visual Services and the Lebanon office of the Social Security Administration, along with retinal specialists, clinical psychologists, and many others. Meeting content added a richness to my life, too. I never regretted the hours I invested in INSIGHT.

The longer Don dealt with blindness the more we understood that his biggest problem was not loss of sight. His biggest problem seemed to be people *with* sight. Every day we saw evidence of sighted people's awkwardness in the presence of the blind. Over the years we accumulated scores of examples of well-meaning friends, acquaintances, and strangers who offered to help in nonsensical ways.

One of the funniest situations occurred with Bob, a hospital administrator. He and Don were going to the same community meeting, and Bob invited to take Don along with him. As the two approached his vehicle Bob said, "There. I'll open the door for you. Then you can get in." Don pondered what he told him, then replied, "That's great, Bob. Where's the car?" When Bob realized what he'd done, he was embarrassed. To help him save face, Don laughed heartily. But we assumed this man learned something important that day.

Not every interaction with sighted folks was funny. Some involved serious judgment. On weekdays Don and I ate lunch together in the hospital snack bar. Afterwards he typically used the lavatory in the hallway heading back to the volunteer office while I waited outside the door for him. One day I noticed that an exceptionally long period of time had passed since he had gone in. Just as I began to wonder if there was a problem, he opened the door, his face burning with anger. I asked him what had happened. The story infuriated me. As Don washed his hands, a man had stepped close to him, invading his personal space. A deep voice inquired if he was blind. Don replied yes. The man pressed on by asking what had caused his loss of vision. When Don told him that long-term diabetes had caused his blindness, the man accused him of being a terrible sinner and commanded him to get down on his knees right there in the men's room and pray for God to restore his sight. Almost hissing, Don advised him to get out of his way before he picked up his cane. It was a bad scene. Obviously to some folks blindness had moral as well as medical implications.

This incident and others burdened Don with guilt. During six years of blindness he heard many unfair—and inaccurate—accusations. In fact, he came to expect them. While he dismissed them intellectually, he harbored them emotionally. I knew there were moments when he questioned if he truly was a good person. This made me sad.

One year after launching INSIGHT the Lebanon Lions Club chose Don as the recipient of their annual Good Neighbor Award. Clearly he'd set an example of how a person could do something positive with a bad deck of cards. In March of 1983 we attended a special dinner hosted by the Lions at a local hotel. The next day a sizable article and photo appeared in the newspaper. The awards committee had selected Don because of the work he'd been doing with other blind people. A former state senator assisted with presenting the plaque. The occasion was special for both of us. Aside from its personal significance, it appeared to seal the relationship between Don and the Lions Club.

Exactly two years later that friendly relationship cracked. After reflecting on a demeaning conversation he'd endured with a young boy downtown in late 1983, Don initiated direct opposition to the Lions Club's annual "white cane" drive. White Cane Days, a Lions International fundraiser for many years, was well known in the community. Its main purpose was to increase the general public's awareness of persons with visual impairments and their needs. Lions Club members stood at various locations in Lebanon and at the malls carrying white canes and a container with the logo "Help the Blind." Passersby were asked to make a donation.

When the young boy approached Don (wearing dark sunglasses) on the street corner and asked him if this was where he begged for money, Don's antagonism for this project erupted. Curious about why the child held this assumption, he pursued the topic. The boy replied that he'd seen a bunch of blind men in suits standing on street corners begging. In his mind all blind people were poor, and they were beggars.

After that incident Don decided to survey approximately forty friends and acquaintances to gain their impressions of the Lions Club fundraiser. He asked if they were familiar with the project, and most said they knew of it. Then he inquired about what it made the blind look like to them. Without exception they all commented that it made blind people look like beggars.

Filled with emotion, Don relayed his personal feelings and the impressions of others to a Lions Club member. Bluntly he stated that he found some aspects of the fundraiser disturbing. As a result he was invited to attend a meeting with several officers of the organization. In that meeting he requested that changes be made as to how the fundraiser was conducted. He asked them to consider eliminating the canes, removing the sunglasses from the containers, and altering the logo. His recommendations were met with rigid resistance. A club-wide vote resulted in a refusal to delete or alter any aspect of the process.

At an INSIGHT meeting twenty-one people signed a petition requesting that the Lions Club re-examine this fundraiser and consider what the INSIGHT members believed to be critical changes. It was interesting that the sunglasses were removed from the containers in the 1984 drive. Don viewed that decision as some progress, although no one from the club had discussed it with him.

A number of Lions believed that Don was downgrading their efforts to help blind people and others with compromised vision. They were deeply offended. It wasn't long until these men criticized Don openly and harshly. The Lions Club president at the time issued a statement assuring folks that nothing negative was ever intended with White Cane Days. The canes and logo had symbolized the fundraiser historically and were integral to its success. He reminded the public that the organization existed to serve and that its focus was sight conservation, blindness, and visual impairment. In summary he said that the club regretted any adverse interpretation of the project.

In response Don explained that he never doubted the Lions' motives to do good. Further, he clarified that he never opposed the project as a whole, but would persist in his efforts to change the way it operated. In fact he was determined to see those changes occur during his lifetime. In his opinion the image of the blind was at stake. He resented the belief that blind people must be pitied. He felt an obligation to stop this.

Because most of the dollars raised by the Lions Club supported their Sight Conservation Program, Don suggested that the White Cane Days focus shift to "Help Save Sight," communicating a more accurate message. Rejecting that wording outright, club members chose "Help Stop Blindness" as the new motto. To our knowledge the language Don preferred was never used. During an interview with a newspaper reporter Don asked this rhetorical question: "Why is it that a service organization dedicated to helping the blind won't listen to the blind?"

As a result of Don's disagreement with the Lebanon Lions Club, our lives became very public. Several lengthy articles about the issue appeared in the local paper. People talked. Certain relationships were strained. Private citizens got involved by writing letters to the newspaper's public forum voicing their empathy for Don as a blind man but essentially siding with the Lions Club. One writer, a former Lion, defended the club's recent decision to run the fundraising campaign as they wanted to run it. He implied that Don didn't value the organization's work.

By now Don volunteered forty hours each week in the hospital's hospice program. He'd learned about this program while listening to a radio talk show and decided to inquire about how he might fit into it. When decision-makers fleshed out a role for him, he leaped at the opportunity to make a difference in a new way. Holding down the fort in the office when staff traveled to patients' homes, he answered the phone, took messages, engaged in emotional conversations with family members of the dying, and was a confidential sounding board for the program directors. On a few occasions he accompanied medical staff on home visitations. Quite a few hospital employees thought Don was part of the paid staff. Although we chuckled at this, we also knew that it signified the level of support he provided in that program. In a fifteen-month period he experienced sixty-four deaths. As a vital presence in the hospice office, Don added a personality and offered a service others could not have supplied. The match was ideal.

Over several years Don sought—and was given—at least thirty opportunities to speak to community groups and churches about the purpose of INSIGHT and the problems of blind people. For two decades I kept many of the printed programs and media clippings from evenings with the American Business Women Association, Rotary Club meetings, and religious committees. Don also provided numerous in-service trainings for nurses. I accompanied him to at least 90 percent of those speaking engagements. In most cases he needed a driver, and we needed to present a united front. From the beginning I'd always felt that we were in this together. Of course *this* refers to our situation and the mess it often created. I wanted others to see us as a team.

From the time he lost all of his eyesight Don was a man on a mission. Teaching sighted people how to communicate and interact with the blind gave him a reason to get up in the morning. When he addressed groups, he incorporated real-life stories. Many of these stories recounted situations that had happened to him personally. Colorful and full of detail, the stories drove home key points in his talks. After Don's death folks remembered them. Occasionally they'd stop me on the street or in a store to tell me.

One story involved a woman who approached Don as he prepared to cross a street. The woman stood close behind him and placed her hands on both of his shoulders. When Don asked her what she was doing, she informed him she was going to help him to cross safely. He asked her why she thought she needed to do that. Hearing it as a ridiculous question, in a loud voice she said she could tell he was blind. Before he knew what had happened, she'd grabbed his white cane and started to push him off the curb. Furious, Don instructed her to return his cane and let him go. As she walked away she muttered, "Ungrateful," under her breath. He imagined what she was thinking. Then he walked across the street by himself.

During question and answer sessions at speaking engagements people frequently inquired why Don didn't have a service dog. The response was simple: He failed to qualify. Due to his systemic health problems, he lacked the necessary physical stamina to exercise a large, young dog every day. Many people in our world associated Seeing Eye dogs with the blind. They were perplexed about his use of a white cane. They couldn't understand why anyone would choose an inanimate object over a lovable animal. Until Don explained it, they didn't realize how much care these dogs demand—and deserve—to stay fit. He told folks that individuals awarded service dogs must assume all of the responsibility for them. Spouses and friends were not permitted to help. Staff at the training organizations with whom we'd spoken pointed out that shared responsibility confused the dogs, who had to develop loyalty to only one master. Don wanted a dog, but he knew he'd never get one.

From podiums all over the county Don shared tales of people's visits to our apartment. Friends stopped by to shoot the breeze, as they termed it. If I wasn't home, they assisted with ordinary little tasks such as making coffee, pouring lemonade, putting pretzels in a bowl, or locating cups. On most every occasion they'd set the beverage on a table but fail to inform Don about which table and precisely where it was located on that table. They'd tell him they gathered napkins but neglect to put one in his hand. They'd go to the bathroom and forget to mention they'd left the room. Depending on his mood, sometimes Don laughed about these kinds of things, and other times he complained.

While these friends genuinely wanted to see Don and provide companionship, they didn't stay very long. Privately they confided to me that they found the experience to be suffocating. When they tried to imagine what Don's life was like twenty-four hours a day, seven days a week, they felt sick. They knew they could run away from the world of darkness when the visits ended; they also knew that Don could not escape it.

One of the paradoxes we discovered was that the sighted population both idolizes and fears the blind. More than once we heard folks describe Don as "amazing." Yet these same people shied away, claiming they didn't know what to say to him. It wasn't unusual for people to talk to me directly about what circled around in their heads. After one particular speaking engagement a woman inquired quietly if I could handle Don by myself as we headed out to the parking lot. Once a work colleague asked me if Don ever traced the outline of my face with his hands. I told her he didn't, and that he never touched me any differently after he lost his vision than before he lost it. She seemed disappointed. She reminded me that on television blind people often touched faces as if they were sculpture. "His is not a TV type of blindness," I remarked. She frowned.

Chapter 3

WALKING THROUGH FEAR

Diary Entry, September 1985

Things are deteriorating. I just finished a supper I didn't want. After taking a sleeping pill, Don went to bed early. He hasn't slept for a full night in nearly three weeks. That means I haven't slept either. I desperately need my rest but rarely get it now. My nerves are frayed, my stomach knotted. I don't need a doctor to tell me that my husband is seriously ill. I see the signs. Daily I observe his weakness and fatigue. Just this morning the simple act of shaving depleted him. Some outside force seems to be sucking the energy out of his body. I feel guilty for asking him to do little routine chores. The diabetes is winning.

I'm exhausted. This isn't a good time for me to make sense of complicated matters. But I find that writing in a journal helps me organize my thoughts and manage my feelings. I need to do something constructive to clarify what's going on inside of me. I need an outlet for the anxiety and fear. It's not fair to dump it on Don. Sometimes I wish I could speed up the dying process—and then hate myself for thinking it. Other times I wish for thousands of hours between this moment and the death. There are days when I have no idea what I want.

I'm discovering that dying can take a long time. In a drive-through society, that's a bitter pill to swallow. It's the long, drawn-

out road to death that takes the biggest toll on patient and partner.
I don't doubt that I can handle death. It's the waiting and wonder-
ing. I'm afraid to let Don go, yet I know he wants to die. For him life
has lost its luster. I stare at him when he doesn't realize I'm there.
His skin is a sickly shade of pale, his lips dry and white. Depression
has flattened his facial expression. Every day there is less and less
of the person I knew. Occasionally I give him valium to calm his
nerves. I've noticed mood swings and memory lapses. I see his swol-
len feet, an indication that circulation is poor. He tells me his legs
hurt. Chest pains from angina come and go, and blood tests show
that his kidneys are starting to fail. I am afraid of the physical and
psychological changes, curious about what it will be like living with
a stranger.

In those dark days fear followed me everywhere. Others didn't see it, but I knew it was there. I'd felt enormous fear when Don lost his vision, but this fear was different. A kind of fear I'd never known before, it was overwhelming. I'd read in a book once that we must admit the possibility of what we fear most; that we are to walk up to the fear and look it full in the face. Realist that I was, I was willing to do that. But my fear didn't have one focus. It had many. And one bled into the others. Thus attending to all of my fears was like working a part-time job.

After twenty-three years of living with diabetes Don had been termed a *brittle diabetic* by specialists. That meant achieving tight control of his blood sugar was almost impossible. In the late summer of 1985 Don asked me to take over his insulin injections. This process happened each morning before breakfast. It involved drawing insulin into a syringe and releasing it slowly beneath the surface of his skin. Because his finger dexterity had dwindled, he no longer trusted his ability to do it correctly. In addition, as a result of more than two decades of sticking himself, the skin on his arms and legs had toughened to the point where it had become difficult to pierce it in the usual areas. He needed someone who could see to select new areas (such as his belly) and hit the mark the first time around. When I first started doing this I feared making mistakes. Since too much insulin could have killed him and too little wouldn't have covered his food intake, I double- and triple-checked the dosage before giving him the shots. Not wanting to hurt him, I found that I winced as I stuck the needle into the chosen site. However, in a few months I'd developed enough skill to handle the entire process with a certain amount of confidence and ease.

By mid-September of 1985 Don entered another phase of the disease. He began to nosedive into serious insulin shocks. These shock episodes, evidence of low blood sugar, always caught us by surprise. Unfortunately there wasn't much to do to prevent them. One afternoon at the close of the business day Don started to sweat profusely in the volunteers' office. Diane, the director, rushed to the snack bar for orange juice and a box of chocolate milk. Frightened, she phoned me at my desk down the street to give me the news. I stopped what I was doing and ran the block to the main hospital building. When I arrived I found Don slumped in his chair, white as a ghost, with beads of perspiration dotting his forehead. I took him home and gave him a sandwich. Then I dressed him in pajamas and helped him into bed. The next day I thought he looked much better.

Six weeks later as I assisted him with casting his ballot during an election at the local firehouse, I noticed his hands shaking. Within seconds the tops of them felt wet to the touch, and sweat dripped visibly from his face and hair. We barely got out of the voting area and into the parking lot before he became so weak that I wondered if he was capable of putting himself into the car. As he struggled to maneuver onto the seat, I realized that a time might come when he wouldn't be able to do it. Don weighed 180 pounds then. I wondered how long I could manage him alone. At home I somehow pulled him out of the car and held him upright against my body as we staggered into the apartment. Hastily I took off his shoes and soaked shirt, then virtually poured a glass of juice down his throat. Don didn't usually eat pastries, but I also gave him a donut. I had to raise his blood sugar as fast as possible. Completely wiped out, he collapsed into his recliner. In our bedroom I cried.

Seven days later he called me at work at 8:30 AM. Not feeling up to going to the hospital, he'd decided to rest at home. When I heard his voice, I knew there was trouble. He proceeded to tell me he'd fallen to the kitchen floor and that he thought he was shocking again. "Please hurry," he said. On autopilot, I sped down the road. As I unlocked the door, I had no idea what I'd find. Once inside, I saw him sitting on a chair by the phone, hunched over the kitchen table. He explained that he'd crawled there after drinking some juice. With tears in his eyes he apologized for not putting the pitcher back in the fridge—he didn't trust himself to walk. Looking at him I observed a man who appeared like he'd just stepped out of the shower. I insisted that he eat a sandwich and a piece of fresh fruit. Once he devoured the food, I washed him and tucked him into bed for a nap. Unnerved, I returned to work.

Fear of these shocks clung to me like a fly on a pest strip. Until his death I was never free of that fear. Even at night I carried it deep in my brain. On occasion I thought I heard Don calling my name, trying to tell me he was in yet another traumatic circumstance. But when I turned to face him and saw him sleeping, I knew I'd imagined it, and relief washed over me. I certainly didn't imagine the scene one early December afternoon at 4:30 as he walked toward me on the pavement and nearly fell. We were on our way to the car. Before starting the motor I fished around in my tote bad for the opera fudge I'd purchased from a colleague. I pressed a couple of pieces into the palm of his hand and ordered him to eat it. This shock was more severe than the one two weeks before. It was harder for me to bring him out of it. But something else accompanied the familiar physical symptoms that time: harsh words and a nasty tone from the man who loved me. As I attempted to wipe the perspiration from his face, he pushed my hand away and told me to stop fussing. He was tired of my need to help.

Christmas came and went. Despite the dawn of a new year, I believed we had little to look forward to except an increasingly slippery slope. That slope was getting steeper by the month. In part I measured the steepness by the severity of the shocks. On January 8th I drove into the circle in front of the hospital. I noticed a volunteer leading Don toward the car. Suddenly my senses soared into high alert. Something was wrong. Peering more closely, I discerned that Don had difficulty following the woman. His legs seemed to be immobile. When I questioned him about it on the way home, he told me he didn't feel well. In the driveway he wasn't talking to me at all. Leaving him in the car, I hurried into the kitchen for orange juice and Karo syrup. Gripped by both the cold and my fear, I went outside and with wooden fingers pried his lips open far enough to insert what I regarded as sugar salvation. There I stood in twenty-degree weather, the wind howling around me, watching my husband perched on the high wire between diabetic coma and viable life. Back in the apartment it felt like hours until he spoke. I stood at his recliner waiting, my neck and shoulders rigid.

By the spring of 1986 Don had become abnormally weak. Others noticed it, too. Diane confided to me that he lacked the strength to climb into the hospital van that transported a group of volunteers to the Volunteer Recognition Luncheon in May. That same month Don announced one evening that he pondered suicide but doubted that he would try it in case he failed. I was cooking dinner at the stove when he told me that. I whirled around to face him, totally stunned. I had never regarded Don as someone who would throw in the towel in such a dramatic way. In a steady voice I asked him about methods he'd considered. Frozen with fear, I heard him admit to the possibility of deliberately dropping his electric razor in the bathroom sink filled with water after I'd gone to work. As if I'd stepped outside of myself, I also heard about his desire to swallow an entire bottle of sleeping pills or stop taking insulin. I stayed silent, unsure what to say. Secretly I realized that a different sort of fear emerged as a result of this conversation. From that day forward I never knew if I'd come home and find him lying on the floor—dead. Although we didn't discuss this topic again, I didn't forget. To cope I filed it in the back of my mind.

According to my memory, the worst of the insulin shock events occurred in October, approximately five months before Don's death. He had been absent from the hospital for over four months and from INSIGHT for five. Because I hadn't slept all night, I'd decided to stay home on this particular morning. At 6:00 AM Don shook my arm, trying to communicate distress. After jumping up and giving him two glasses of juice I assessed his blood sugar with the compact machine we'd purchased at the pharmacy. Relatively new technology, this machine provided a fairly accurate blood glucose reading. At that moment the dashboard indicated a mere "68." (The accepted normal range was between 80 and 120 in the 1980s.) I could have screamed. A higher number should have popped up on that screen.

Kneeling by the side of the bed, I stared at the blue pajamas pasted to Don's shivering body. They were drenched. I watched more sweat pore from his head, neck, and chest. When he didn't answer me when I called his name, I spoke loudly and continuously to keep him awake. Eventually he consumed several peanut butter crackers and a big glass of milk. After he fell asleep, I lay down beside my husband and simply listened to myself breathe. Another crisis had passed. I wondered how many more were in store for us.

Among the folks in our world who were aware of these episodes, many questioned why something could not be done to prevent them or reduce their frequency. Some implied that perhaps Don was eating too many high-calorie foods, sneaking the wrong foods, and/or taking too much insulin. Some questioned the doctor's prescription and judgment. This frustrated me because I understood how people who are considered brittle diabetics can shock after big meals and can run high sugars when their stomachs are empty. I saw evidence of it with Don. Logically, though, the craziness made no sense to laypeople.

What was it about those awful shocks that horrified me? I didn't want him to die. Digging deeper, I suspected that I didn't want him to die *like that*—a semiconscious "half person," sweating like a pig, unable to speak. If he was going to die, I wanted him to do so with at least a tad of dignity. And yes, if I am to be completely honest, I didn't want someone in the medical community to blame me for not doing the right thing in a situation we'd experienced over and over again. I didn't want medical personnel or our friends and acquaintances to doubt my ability to rise to the occasion and save him one more time. I needed to appear competent.

In June of that year another complication of long-term diabetes reared its ugly head. I came home from work to discover that Don's speech was slurred and he couldn't form words easily, a heaviness holding his tongue hostage. Upon further examination I noticed his poor coordination and the dragging of his left leg. We guessed he'd suffered a small stroke known as a transient ischemic attack, or TIA. From conversations with doctors and my own reading about the progression of diabetes we knew this TIA would not be the last. I especially worried about the situation because Don still smoked a couple of cigarettes each day. Since smoking narrows blood vessels, I harbored anger about the habit he hadn't beaten. A few weeks prior to this incident he'd burned a hole in a cloth place mat on the kitchen table. He'd lost control of the lighted cigarette, and it had fallen from his fingers. Fortunately I had been present in the room. As I thought about the likelihood of more mini-strokes in the future, I feared what could happen if one came over him while smoking alone. I shivered.

My worst fear became a reality on an evening when I attended a women's group meeting in a nearby town. Returning home around 9:00, I heard Don call my name from the kitchen in a sheepish tone. He proceeded to tell me that he'd dropped a cigarette on the floor and couldn't find it. My heart pounded. I imagined him stepping on a fiery tip in bare feet. It wasn't long before I located the object of discussion in a corner. Lying in bed later, I kept thinking about what happened and how things might have turned out differently had I not arrived when I had. Although he hadn't suffered a TIA that night, he had dropped a lighted cigarette. It could have landed on his pants. The rest would have been history.

At the end of June I was busy preparing Sunday supper when I heard a thud in the living room followed by a crash. Abandoning the spaghetti sauce, I ran to see what was going on. Don lay face down on the carpet, the lamp table cockeyed against the wall. His radio and ash tray had flown off the table and landed behind the recliner. Disoriented and weak, Don, thankfully, was not seriously hurt. A few brush burns marked his elbows and knees. That was all. But I couldn't lift him to his feet. I turned him over and suggested he lie on his back on the floor until he was able to stand up by himself. For perhaps fifteen minutes I knelt beside him. Had he lost his balance when he got off the chair, or did he have another small stroke? We never knew.

Chapter 4

MOVING FORWARD

Don's dying process was the most immense thing I'd ever known. In the pit of my stomach I sensed its onset months before a physician officially informed us, yet that inner knowing didn't make October 20th, 1986, any easier. "You have three to twelve months to live," the nephrologist said gravely during the ninety-minute consult. "Your kidneys are failing as a result of long-term juvenile diabetes. You will experience increasing weakness and eventually acute nausea. You might become bedridden. I advise you to organize your will and insurance policies now. I'm sorry to tell you that we've reached the end of the line medically. Dialysis or a kidney transplant is not a viable option for you given the physical and psychosocial complications. Besides, I know you don't want dialysis. As a physician, my goal is to lower your blood pressure and keep you as comfortable as possible. I'm so sorry."

For many weeks I had expected to hear those words. Yet when I finally heard them, I was stunned. Frequently I replayed the scenario in my mind, completely overwhelmed by it. Listening to the doctor's words in real time, my mouth felt like somebody had stuffed it full of cotton. My jaw tightened from tension. Understanding the necessity of asking practical questions, I took control of myself so I could obtain the information I needed. I had to. I was going to be the chief caregiver. To anyone watching, I probably appeared calm. My hands lay folded neatly in my lap. I didn't cry. I simply sat there on the chair next to Don and absorbed the fatal news. Out of the side of my eye I noticed a blank expression on his face. I had no idea what he was thinking.

When we arrived home I cooked a small supper. Not long after he finished eating Don vomited his meal in the bathroom. I regarded the purging as a delayed response to the devastating news. Then I helped him into bed. A few hours later when I crawled in beside him, I wished I could pull the covers over my head forever. I wanted time to stop. Mentally I resisted the platter of pain that had been handed to me earlier that day. I wanted to avoid it, discard it, jump over it. Anything but embrace it.

I discovered quickly that anticipatory grief—roller coaster that it is—is a unique burden. It grabbed me by the throat and squeezed hard in those weeks and months leading up to the final event. I couldn't shake it off. There were moments when it choked me and caused me to doubt my ability to endure. It felt like a stranger had invaded my body and mind without my permission. One day I was angry, the next day lonely, despite frequent contacts from friends. Simmering anxiety prevented or interrupted sleep, leaving me fuzzy-brained and irritable. I obsessed over details that needed my attention, struggling to avoid mistakes that could cost time, money, or relationships. Sometimes I felt guilty for not doing more to increase Don's physical and psychic comfort. Sometimes a paralyzing dread of the future washed over me as I tried to imagine myself in the bed alone in an empty house. During that period I was very hard on myself, always questioning if I was being and doing enough.

I also wondered what Don remembered about me physically. Six years into his blindness he said he'd forgotten the details of my body. He told me he knew I was tall and that my hair was brown and my eyes were grey. But he couldn't recall my features in his mind. It had been too long since he had seen them. That admission, which had come out of the blue, unnerved me. During his dying I accepted that I'd been reduced to a generic pair of hands needed primarily to nurse, to cook, to clean. Don never said that. He never even implied it. It was something I sensed.

Looking back, this phase was a gift despite its trials. It gave me the opportunity to start getting used to the idea of death and all that accompanies it. It gave me the chance to find meaning in my husband's suffering as well as my own. It gave me the time to identify and grieve for each individual loss I or we experienced—the obvious losses of health and mobility, of course, and more subtle losses like peace of mind, typical marital function, freedom, and fun, to name a few. Personally I grieved the fact that my role of caregiver trumped my role as wife.

I also grieved my loss of blissful sleep. Eventually my sleeplessness evolved into a relentless chronic insomnia. It became a kind of hell. One night at 3:00 AM I wrote a poem to create something constructive out of the pain.

Insomnia

In the darkness of the night
I listen to the clock keep time
    Tick-Tock
The seconds march.

Exhausted
Images of his death loom large in my brain
    and frustrate sleep.
They hover close
    and rob me of peace.
A calculated torture
I cannot cry.
I am drowning in grief
    born of cruel knowledge.

Life now is one endless day
    promising no relief
Until the thief finally claims him who suffers.

Morning will come.

Despite my fatigue, I flew into action after the prognostic doctor visit. During a break at work I phoned one of our closest friends to deliver the news. When she asked what she could do, I suggested that she phone Don just to chat. No longer volunteering at the hospital since the beginning of October, he was home alone while I was at work. Time hung heavy for him. I encouraged her to call him regularly, explaining that he got lonely sitting there for eight hours a day in a quiet apartment. I contacted other friends, too, communicating the same message. Everyone wanted to help, but they depended on me to tell them how.

Over lunch I stopped by the hospice office on the hospital campus. I wanted to know exactly what paid and unpaid staff could do for us when the situation deteriorated beyond my capability. The director assured me that I didn't need to do everything by myself. At the end of our discussion she hugged me and said, "When you and Don are ready for us, let me know. We'll send in the troops." Leaving the building, I felt a certain relief.

Back at work I requested to speak with my supervisor privately. I told her I didn't know precisely what to expect going forward, but that I might need a little time off here and there or even full days. Together we discussed options for dealing with the mountain of patient files that were my responsibility if and when I was absent. We agreed that one of my colleagues should be trained.

Later that day I drove to the Visiting Nurse Association across town to inform the manager that I might have to tap their services. I inquired about scheduling, equipment availability, and fees. I stressed that Don fully intended to control his situation until he no longer could do so. Upon hearing that, the woman recommended a gradual introduction to their agency as the need arose. "Right now I think it's best to involve your friends, because they are people your husband already knows," she advised. I nodded to acknowledge her point. No question about it; Don was going to be a tough nut when it came to bringing health care personnel into our home. Trying to convince him of its value to both of us would be a challenge. He wanted only me.

Throughout the next couple of weeks I told the human resources director and some of my coworkers about Don's terminal status. I received mixed reactions ranging from sadness to utter disbelief. One of the women shared highlights of her first husband's dying process from cancer. When I asked her what it was like for her, she kept repeating the word *frightening* in a voice overcome with emotion. She had three little children to raise on her own. At least I didn't have that responsibility. Communicating my news to others temporarily calmed my nerves. There was something therapeutic about recounting the story over and over. For those few minutes the telling desensitized my brain to a truth too ugly to bear.

In November my only living grandmother sent me a four-page letter in which she first expressed concern for our situation and then went on to describe her sixty years of marriage to my grandfather. "We were happy together," she wrote. "He was a good mate: hard working, cooperative, and a good provider. But somewhere along the line I came to compare life to a bouquet of roses. While the flowers are beautiful, there are thorns among them. Paul had so many difficult surgeries followed by complications. The last straw was his diagnosis of intestinal cancer which, as you know, snuffed out his life. During his final year I lost thirty-six pounds. Some nights I got only an hour's sleep. But when we married, we promised to take care of each other forever. So I honored that promise as he lay dying. It wasn't easy. Life is what you make it." How touching those words were from a woman many regarded as stiff and cold.

Her letter supported my resolve to keep going. If Grandma could do the heavy lifting, then so could I. In fact, I wondered if it might be easier for me—less taxing—because I was decades younger than she when our avalanche hit. Though that assumption proved to be wrong, it had crossed my mind more than once.

Despite nerve-racking blood sugar swings, body tremors and bowel problems caused by neuropathy, unexplained dizzy spells, and an ever-present limp, Don occasionally enjoyed playing the game *Trivial Pursuit* in the evenings. This seemed to be one of his few remaining joys in life. It was something he could do without eyesight. I tried to make time for it. When we played, he concentrated on the questions instead of on his problems. In the middle of a game one night near Halloween he said to me, "You're stronger now than I am." This comment came out of nowhere. A few moments passed until I agreed that I was physically stronger. "No, you are stronger than I am in every way," he said.

The next evening he called the funeral home to inquire about the cost of cremation. That morning I'd kept an appointment with the hospital's employee relations office to inform folks there that I might need a leave of absence from my job to care for my husband. I told them that things were winding down and I didn't know how long I could take care of him and meet my employment obligations. I relayed highlights from the recent visit with the nephrologist. My account of the situation was received with both empathy and denial. One of the human resource specialists, a registered nurse by profession, looked at me and said that Don's doctors didn't really know him and his stubborn resolve to live. She went on to say that Don might end up beating the disease. I gulped.

At some point during the month of November the spiritual journey Don had traveled throughout the year culminated in a decision to join my church. Completely his choice, it caught me by surprise. Admittedly I influenced his thinking, as we frequently discussed spiritual matters. But I never prodded him to follow my lead. In fact I didn't expect him to do anything formally with the beliefs he held. When he told me he wanted to become a member of the church before 1986 ended, I offered to set the logistical balls in motion. Immediately I contacted my priest and we scheduled Don's reception into the Catholic Church for the beginning of December. The ceremony took place in our living room. By then Don was too weak and too wobbly to leave the apartment. In my presence and that of four trusted friends he made his commitment. I had not seen my husband that happy in two years.

A couple of weeks later we celebrated Don's forty-fourth and final birthday. To my relief the morning began with a reasonably normal blood sugar value. By 11:00 AM ten cards in the mailbox and a fresh fruit basket delivered to our door brought a little smile to his pasty, puffy face. Friends and family had remembered the occasion. In the afternoon he lay in his recliner with his feet up and listened for hours to many of the cassette tapes he'd produced on various subjects over the course of the fall. I had mixed feelings about his spending his birthday dwelling on diabetes, blindness, and death, but I soon assessed that this was what he preferred to do. I'd known that these tapes were intended to be his most important legacy. Don desperately wanted other people to benefit from his personal experiences described in detail in the recordings. He also hoped that I'd write about them someday. Privately I thought the tapes had provided a much-needed focus as well as preserving his sanity during the hours he was alone. After completing each one, he'd felt a sense of accomplishment.

The Christmas season brought a flood of visitors—hospital administrators and volunteers, Don's father, neighbors, my father and his wife, members of INSIGHT, and our closest friends. In a few cases Don informed people of his terminal diagnosis for the first time. Reactions varied. Some cried; others didn't know what to say. One man said how glad he was Don had told him, because a man can't keep something that big to himself without breaking. It was true that the telling released tension.

As much as he accepted his decline, Don confessed to me privately that he didn't want to die. He told me over lunch one day that he'd spent two hours just bathing and shaving that morning. He laid down his sandwich mechanically. All of a sudden he put his head in his hands and said loudly, "Shit, I'm dying, Sylvia," with such force it spun my head around. It felt like I'd been slapped. The tone of finality in his voice shocked me. I found it difficult to go back to work.

A few days after Christmas we drove to the podiatrist for a routine appointment. As a person with diabetes, Don thought regular foot care was important. In early 1986 he'd had an ulcer on one toe, and we'd healed it using special ointment. During this visit the doctor casually commented on a slight rubbing together of two toes. She told us it was nothing to worry about at the time. However, it wasn't long until the rubbing produced a sore. Understanding the need for intervention, I requested a prescription for a topical antibiotic. Five weeks later I noticed a small amount of inflammation on another toe as I helped Don put on his socks. This inflammation indicated that the problem was getting worse, not better. Another call to the medical practice led to doubling the topical antibiotic and introducing betadine foot soaks before and between treatments. I got out of bed every morning at 5:00 to start those soaks before I showered and dressed for work.

Within forty-eight hours Don could not walk on the foot with the sore toe. I phoned his regular doctor who insisted on examining him. As soon as he saw the spreading inflammation, he recommended an inpatient stay in the hospital. Intravenous antibiotics had to be administered to combat the infection. While Don balked at the idea of being admitted, he realized he had no choice if he wanted to avoid amputation. Reluctantly he consented to the only sensible course of action.

Forty-eight hours on IV antibiotics slightly improved the situation, allowing us to be hopeful despite the fact that the drug had caused more damage to Don's already malfunctioning kidneys. To our surprise, a surgeon, upon inspection of the toe, voiced his strong opinion that ultimately Don would not escape amputation. He said we could try to control the inflammation at home, but he doubted that we'd succeed. He was right. At the end of February we faced readmission to the hospital, and the toe came off. The surgery itself went well. The best part for me was that Don accepted it.

Once at home Don experienced significant pain in his foot. For days I dressed the wound where the amputation had occurred. When he tried to walk, he hobbled. Clearly the surgery had affected his balance. I suggested a walker to aid his mobility around our apartment. He didn't argue.

What he resisted was help from hospice. Venting to a social worker on the phone, I told her about Don's adamant unwillingness to cooperate with the program resources available to him. I proposed that his fifteen months in the hospice office was now actually working against him. And us. As a volunteer he'd learned up close that death doesn't happen only to other people—it would happen to him, too. Now death had become personal. It was no longer about former hospice patients. It was about him—Don. He didn't want to be on the receiving end of services because they would rub his nose in his own imminent demise.

For several days we muddled through the emerging daily challenges on our own. Don was quiet and distant, staring blankly into space, apparently absorbed in his own thoughts. I viewed his behavior as a sign of emotional retreat from the world. After a friend visited, she called me to share her observations. "I was disappointed to find that the feisty Don is gone," she said. "I think he's giving up. I never guessed he'd do that." Taking a deep breath, I suggested that he wasn't giving up but giving in to the inevitable. Fighting prolonged the misery. She didn't want to hear this and hung up.

Chapter 5

ACKNOWLEDGING MY FEELINGS

I remember the times when people asked us directly if we really wanted to know that Don was going to die. Don told them that nobody *wants* to know, but they need to know. He believed that folks deserve to know the truth in order to prepare for death. I believed it, too. We'd discovered that there were things to say and things to do in whatever time was left. Important things.

At 2:00 AM on March 2nd I awoke to the noise of violent vomiting followed by moans and sobs. Immediately I noticed that Don wasn't in bed. Sometime during the night he'd moved to avoid disturbing me. I jumped up and switched on the ceiling lamp in the hall. The disturbing sounds came from the bathroom. Thin yellow lines of light illumined the silhouette of a sick man kneeling tightly against the commode, his hands gripping the seat. I saw the sweat glistening on his forehead. Breathing heavily, I tried to absorb the scene before me.

I wiped Don's face and flushed the toilet. Unexpectedly his head bumped my hand, and he leaned deeply into the bowl. He retched until he was weak. Dry heaves overpowered him. I felt dizzy from fear and fatigue. Once he looked up at me, pleading for help. In a little while I cleaned him with warm, soapy water. Somehow I raised him up from the floor, but he collapsed against my chest. Slowly I led him to his recliner in the living room where he sank like dead weight into the cushion. His pajamas were wet, his body cold.

Waves of nausea came and went. I placed a bucket by his chair. When he was able to talk, Don urged me to go back to sleep. In our bed I tossed and turned. I never slept. I listened. By dawn he began to hyperventilate. I expected dehydration or shock. Or both. While I didn't need a doctor to tell me he was in trouble, I had to call.

When I reached Don's regular doctor, he decided to order blood tests to check renal function. Not surprising, Don was too weak to dress or walk. Paramedics, after accidentally ramming his sore foot into a porch post on the way to the ambulance, transported him to the emergency room. I followed in my car. Once we arrived, the intense vomiting commenced again. Despite an injection of anti-nausea medication, he wretched on the gurney for hours. To my surprise some nurses honestly believed the vomiting resulted from acute anxiety. I was furious. I knew my husband's kidneys were failing. At noon Don bolted upright, spewing bile like a geyser all over my pants, stockings, and shoes. I nearly gagged. Still, staff and I worked as a team, placing metal trays under Don's chin. I watched in horror as he heaved and cried.

Medical personnel in the cardiac care unit finally stabilized the situation by 6:00 PM. Part of the treatment included intravenous nitroglycerin because doctors suspected the onset of a coronary due to heart rhythm changes. It had been an agonizingly long day for both of us. Exhausted, I went home to change clothes, then ate supper with close friends. I chewed the food but didn't taste it. Later that evening I learned that Don's red blood cell count was low and the toe infection had spread. Doctors had scheduled multiple blood transfusions for the next day and held serious discussions about amputating the left foot or even the leg. In the meantime exceptionally potent antibiotics dripped into Don's veins as a last-ditch effort to save the limb. I went to bed numb, wondering how long I'd hold up under the strain.

At the crack of dawn on March 6th Don phoned me at home to complain about nausea. I showered, dressed, and drove purposefully to the hospital. When I walked into his room on the second floor, I found him sitting on the side of the bed looking pale and sick. I pulled up a chair and spoke softly. The more I talked, the more he calmed down. While I went to the office, he lay for hours, lost in a world no one could share. That evening I held his hand, a thousand "what ifs" clogging my head like sludge.

The following day, a Saturday, I spent the morning with Don. A nurse and I bathed him in bed. He ate a full breakfast and lunch. A few friends visited. Everyone remarked how his disposition had improved. To them he seemed more like good old Don. I allowed myself to relax.

I awakened on Sunday, March 8th, 1987, to warm, bright sunshine after uninterrupted sleep. The three elderly unmarried sisters who'd become aunts to me suggested that I join them for lunch at their home. The dining room, flooded with light, resembled a garden with fresh green plants artfully positioned among pink and blue violets in their large, triple, white-curtained window. Several poinsettias left over from Christmas sat on the hardwood floor in the corners. Pushing guilt from my mind, I decided to enjoy the meal. I had no idea what was going on at the hospital. But I chose to revel in the loveliness of a lace tablecloth, delicate china dishes, and stemmed goblets for an hour or two. There, surrounded by these loving women, I felt mothered and safe.

Studying Don after I arrived at the hospital in the early afternoon, I recognized signs of confusion. Agitated, he insisted I'd taken him to another town and another place. I wondered if he was septic or had suffered a stroke. As the day progressed he became extremely restless. He constantly crawled in and out of bed, unable to achieve a satisfactory level of comfort. Family and friends stopped by, and his energy level waxed and waned. With some folks he conversed; with others he stayed silent. In the pit of my stomach I sensed something about to happen. Nervously I asked a nurse to report the results of the latest kidney studies. They were poor, the worst they could get. Amputation of the leg had been scheduled for the following morning, exactly one week after Don's admission. Bluntly I was told there was no other choice. The nurses at the desk avoided eye contact. They knew this was a bad situation and that I was running out of steam.

Around 8:00 PM I covered my husband's body with a blanket and encouraged him to sleep. As I stood in the doorway looking back at him stretched out in the middle of the bed, I told him I loved him and promised to return in the morning. Although I didn't realize it then, those were my last words to him. I went home, barely able to stand from fatigue.

At 9:00 PM the ring of the telephone jarred me. I'd been writing in my diary, determined to capture details from the day. The physician on call for Don's medical practice greeted me by my first name. His voice was deep and severe. I'd guessed the reason for his call. When he informed me officially of Don's death from cardiac arrest triggered by renal failure, he could not have predicted the impact of his message. I heard it as if I'd been totally unaware for two years that Don was going to die. I heard it as shocking information communicated to someone outside of myself. My arms and legs stiffened. My fingers shook. My mouth went dry. It was so dry I could barely talk. Somehow I thanked him for contacting me and assured him I would go back to the hospital shortly. For legal purposes I needed to identify the body.

A friend from work drove me in her car. Neither of us cried. Our jaws were tight as we rode the elevator. It's interesting that no doctors were visible when we arrived on Don's floor. The hallway, deserted and dim, was eerily quiet. Only a ward clerk manned the nursing station; she didn't look up as we passed. Slowly, with feet of wood, I approached the door to my husband's room. My friend waited outside as I pushed open the door. I didn't know what to expect.

Our priest stood on the far side of the bed, and Don's sister and her husband occupied the foot. I saw the three of them before I dared to glance at Don. His face had turned an ugly shade of purple and red, especially the cheek pressed against the pillow. Only forty-five minutes had gone by since the doctor's call. Obviously physical changes were already underway. I'd read about women who touched and clung to their husbands' bodies, hardened by death. I didn't want to do that. I didn't need to do that. I stared briefly, then left.

I had no interaction with medical or hospital staff that night. It was as if they had chosen to dodge me. I decided it really didn't matter. My friend took me home and lay beside me until I fell asleep sometime after 1:00 AM.

The next morning at the church our priest helped me plan Don's Memorial Mass. We sat in his office, me on the sofa and he in his big chair, pen and tablet in hand. For more than an hour we discussed many things, including my eulogy and Don's wish for us to play one of his cassette tapes specifically designated for this occasion. I struggled to focus, my eyes puffy from too many tears. Once the priest looked up at me over his glasses and asked how I was feeling. I told him I thought I might crumble. Smiling thinly he said, "I know *you* too well. *You* won't crumble. You will go on. But your life will change. I just don't know how." I carried those words with me for months.

Several days passed in a blur. They were filled with obligations and errands such as picking up the suitcase of Don's clothes at the hospital and a packet of death certificates at the funeral home. I was disappointed to learn that the funeral director refused to visit my apartment. On the ride home I wept until I scarcely could see the road. In our bedroom I unpacked the case, rubbing the pajamas Don wore when he died against my nose. As I smelled my husband's scent in the material, he seemed near. My youngest sister from Indiana was staying with me now, and together we put everything away in Don's drawers. I wasn't ready to part with it. What I trashed was twenty-five bottles of pills. With pleasure I flushed them all down the toilet.

Flowers, cards, and condolence letters arrived at my door in rubber-banded bundles. The card that meant the most to me came from the president of the Lebanon Lions Club. He wrote that despite their clash about the white cane fundraiser, he'd always admired Don for his convictions and his courage. Someone else wrote that he and his wife had been impressed with our relationship and boldness, which was not expressed in a grim way but in hardheaded honesty, humor, diverse interests, and a love of life. For me, writing scores of thank-you notes and acknowledgment letters was a welcome chore. Concentrating on personalized messages provided much-needed psychic relief. I penned a note, then addressed an envelope, sealed it, and stamped it before adding it to the carefully arranged pile. This illustrated my need to be methodical while completing simple tasks. In my grief I found comfort in a simple, step-by-step process.

After three days I pulled myself together and returned to work. At the end of my first day back at work I drove once again to the funeral home to retrieve Don's ashes. There I was handed a fifteen-pound can resembling a flour canister. It rode beside me on the passenger seat, reminding me of the evening just four months previously when Don had opted for cremation. At home I placed the can on the kitchen table where it stayed for a few weeks until Don's sister and I finally released the ashes together. The secret Berks County, Pennsylvania, location had been a favorite of Don's during boyhood. We set the tin on a log that afternoon and pried the lid open with a screwdriver. With deliberate determination and dry eyes I lifted the can, shaking its course, ivory bone contents over a small stream. The two of us stood in the mud and watched the ashes cling to the rocks.

At night I lay in bed remembering and reviewing my marriage, especially the final two years. In those early weeks after Don's death I subconsciously imagined him still at the hospital, as if he'd come home when the crisis had passed. This made me feel less alone. According to my diary entries I'd started to feel alone and lonely by the fall of 1985. In the summer of 1986 I wrote that I was gripped by an overwhelming feeling of grief, fear, and anticipation that I couldn't shake and couldn't quite explain. The enormity of the ordeal we faced was fast becoming real. From childhood I'd feared roller coasters, and I knew I was riding one. That reality hit me like a slap.

As early as December of 1985 I privately referred to my state of mind as a "circumstantial depression no one but me could see." I didn't discuss it with others. Of course Don didn't see it, being blind. Thus I was quite successful hiding it from him, too. That depression, however, played out in long periods of silence during some meals, stubborn refusal to attend social events, and quiet, simmering rage. Late at night I sometimes sat on the sofa and cried, slipping into a mood that made me think death was easier than life. In retrospect, mine was very much a functional depression. I got out of bed in the morning no matter how tired I was; I maintained my job no matter how difficult the circumstances; I did whatever had to be done no matter what was required. To those who watched, I appeared like I had everything under control. This was a fact—not my assumption—because some folks told me how they viewed things. While I never used the words *under control* in conversations with colleagues, family, and friends, I appreciated their vote of confidence. Perhaps I needed them to think what they thought—for Don and for me. On a drive once I remarked with anger to a close friend that I was bored with being a nurse and a housewife whose life consisted only of duty and chores. My words dripped with resentment. By saying that I'd stepped outside of the careful lines I'd drawn for myself. Later I regretted it.

I remember a rainy winter morning in 1985 when I stood at the bathroom sink brushing my teeth. Don was asleep in our bed across the hall. As I was about to rinse toothpaste down the drain, I noticed a single drop of water that had splashed along the side of the bowl. Its unusual heart shape caught my eye. A Valentine in January! In that instant I felt warm, as if someone's arms were hugging me. That soft warmth moved into a gentle joy that stayed with me for hours. I felt like I could do anything then.

Occasionally I dreamed dreams that affected me similarly. A couple of weeks before Don's terminal diagnosis I felt my work supervisor's arms around me while I slept. It was as if she had reached out to comfort me in the aftermath of a loss. When I woke up peace washed over me. It was a lovely moment. When I walked into the office later and saw her, I marveled. This woman disliked most of her staff and treated us accordingly. I couldn't imagine her showing me such compassion.

Not all of my dreams were friends. Unpleasant family history emerged as well as themes of serious illness and a strong desire for freedom from the trap that was my world. Frequently I dreamed that Don suffered small strokes, insulin shocks, or falls when I wasn't with him. He cried out to me for help but I didn't hear. Total strangers cared for him until he recovered. Upon waking I felt intense sadness and guilt. Once I dreamed of him lying in an incubator-type crib in a hospital, me standing nearby stroking his head. Many times I woke up feeling like a wind-up toy ready to snap.

Don dreamed too. Six weeks before his actual death he told me at breakfast that he'd died. I asked him how it felt. He said he didn't really know; that he hadn't sensed anything in particular. It was more of an event devoid of emotion or physical sensation. As he told me about it, his voice was flat. On another morning he recounted a different kind of dream about his own death. This one had involved feelings of euphoria because his health had been restored and he could see again. He said he didn't want to wake up. A boyish smile spread across his face. My heart literally skipped a beat.

From the beginning ours had been a conversational marriage. When we were alone we talked about everything: past vacations to faraway places, his fears about dying, our financial affairs, my future life. Often I sat at his feet in the living room as we covered innumerable topics of mutual interest. Our marriage had been peaceful, too. We didn't bicker or abuse like many couples. Although we disagreed about some issues, we talked through them. Don was a principled person, and so am I. That combination made for animated discussions at times. When folks learned after Don's death that we co-existed in a tension-free environment, many expressed surprise. They knew Don as a man who held firm opinions, rarely budging if he thought he was right. They perceived me as a woman who was apt to give in, favoring harmony at home. There was some truth in both assumptions, but not to the extent people believed.

Don cared deeply about me, and he frequently looked for little ways to make me happy despite our circumstances. He sent me flowers for my birthday and Valentine's Day. As long as he could walk without a great deal of difficulty, he shopped for Christmas gifts with Diane. He tried to avoid making a mess in the apartment. For no reason he asked me if I was okay. On most days I felt respected and loved.

Yet Don was demanding as he was dying. If he wanted something done, he wanted it done immediately. As his wife, I was on the receiving end of those demands. When I was tired or busy, I rebelled against them. When I was well-rested I understood that those demands resulted from feeling separated from the mainstream of life and from an awareness of losing control. Occasionally I perceived them as attempts to get my undivided attention. There were evenings when he insisted that I go back to the store for more cassette tapes after I'd brought a pack home. There was a night in the winter of 1987—a few weeks prior to his death—when his fingernail clippers broke at 10:00 and he cried until, totally exasperated, I broke down and drove to the pharmacy for a new one. In Don's dying mind, waiting until morning to buy a replacement wasn't an option.

In the summer of 1986 a top manager at the hospital business office stopped to chat with me in the hall. Studying me intently, he inquired about Don. Then he said, "Your face looks different somehow. I can't put my finger on it. I just know there's something there that wasn't there before." I didn't comment.

Chapter 6

MAKING DECISIONS, MANAGING DILEMMAS

During the course of my marriage I—and we—encountered a bagful of problems after Don lost most of his vision. Upon close examination I realized that some of these problems could be solved and others could not. Among those that could be solved, it was generally a matter of identifying the right resources, then making a decision about how to access them. Among those that could not be solved, it was a matter of recognizing them for what they were: difficult dilemmas that wouldn't go away.

The dilemmas in our lives unquestionably caused the greatest pain. The first dilemma I personally faced focused on the frequency and intensity with which I chose to share my emotions with my husband. Quite early in the game I learned that Don disliked tears. Mine in particular made him insecure. Historically I had been a woman who rarely shed physical tears over anything. But this situation was different. Don's blindness and health deterioration both engulfed and grieved me. Occasionally I cried. Crying didn't change anything; it relieved stress.

Approximately four months prior to his demise Don called me at the office to pass along the results of his most recent kidney function tests. His voice sounded a bit shaky. Two significant numbers had climbed. I swallowed hard and finished the work day. Opening the front door at home, I burst into tears. Don sat in his recliner, his face a stone. At some point he asked me why I was crying and proceeded to say there was no reason for it. In that moment it was clear to me that his acceptance of his death had reached a level mine had not. I walked into the kitchen, refusing to comment. At the sink I ate a couple of cookies, big warm tears sliding silently down my cheeks. Wordlessly I'd just said no to him. My silence and leaving the room meant "No, I am not answering your question because I find it inane."

Saying no to Don was hard. I didn't enjoy setting boundaries with him, yet sometimes I had to do it. I had to do it for me, and I had to do it for him. Standing there at the sink I remembered the first day I had done that. Just back from grocery shopping, I heard his request to take the car for a wash across town. He told me I had enough time before the place closed. Yes, the car was dirty and needed a bath. I sighed. It was a Saturday, and I'd spent hours cleaning until I'd left for the store. I didn't want to go out again. Politely and gently, I informed him that I would get the car washed on Monday. I yearned to stretch out on the sofa and read a book. Though Don didn't argue, he pouted.

One summer evening he insisted on fixing the sliding screen door before dinner. For a while that door hadn't opened easily because the screws were loose. I watched him get down on his hands and knees and struggle to locate the screws at the base of the door. The pathetic scene broke my heart. I offered to help. Obviously he couldn't see what he was doing, but stubbornly he declined. I saw that his legs hurt on that hard kitchen floor, and his frustration mounted. Again I repeated my offer to help if he'd show me what to do. He shook his head. Frantically, with perspiration beading on his forehead, he searched for the screws. Out of desperation he asked me to position the screwdriver in the hole on top of one screw. It took him an undetermined number of minutes to turn the handle until he succeeded in tightening the screw. The process was painstakingly slow. His face dripped sweat, his breathing labored. I worried about his heart.

Unfortunately this tedious job was far from done. Half a dozen more screws needed to be turned. He asked me to assist as I had before. I said no. He had done enough. Not only was the task nearly impossible for someone who was blind, it was taking a notable physical toll. I announced that I would finish the project. In response Don tossed the screwdriver across the tile, irritated by my decision. He literally crawled to the counter to balance his body before attempting to stand. I saw the strain in his face. After three agonizing tries he pulled himself up from the floor. A mental image of the stronger man I'd once known flashed in front of my eyes. I could have wept, but didn't.

After spending another supper talking about serious health issues around Labor Day, 1986, I recommended that we take a hiatus from the topics of illness, dying, and death for a little while. This, too, was a version of saying no. I explained that I couldn't deal with those conversations every day. I thought a break would do us good. Don put his head in his hands and became quiet. I didn't know what was coming. After what seemed to be a very long time he turned towards me and said my suggestion had hurt him deeply. But I held my ground. I needed to preserve my sanity.

Knowing when to push Don and when to let him do things in his own time presented an awkward dilemma for me. Months before *he* decided to travel to the National Federation of the Blind's headquarters in Baltimore I thought he should have made that commitment. His eyesight had been diminishing significantly. The situation resembled a snowball rolling downhill, gathering momentum as each month passed. I firmly believed he needed to learn to live as a blind man, the sooner the better. He wasn't able to teach himself. He required outside instruction and guidance from professionals who lived with blindness every day. Though I witnessed the grief in him, I decided not to press. If I'd forced him to do something he wasn't ready to do, he'd have hated me. That wouldn't have helped our marriage.

As Don's health deteriorated, he frequently asked me to stay home from work. He felt less lonely and more secure when I was there with him. Even during periods of silence as he napped or escaped into happy memories, he liked having me near. The problem was that I couldn't play hooky on a regular basis. I had to keep my job. We needed my paycheck, but most especially the benefits. Discerning when to go and when to stay never got easier. If Don had suffered a severe insulin shock during the night, I usually chose to take off, tapping my bank of paid leave. If I sensed that he was physically stable but emotionally fragile, I went to the office an hour late. I'd established simple criteria in order to make up my mind. I didn't honor all of his requests to stay home. There were too many of them over the course of a year. Once at my desk, though, I'd second-guess my decision every time.

An upsetting scene before work would get my day off to a rocky start. As I'd drive to the hospital I'd play it over and over in my head, wondering if I'd made the right choice. Nagging gremlins whispered that I'd be sorry if something bad happened to him. Those gremlins plagued me until he died. Even then a few hung around and tormented me with subtle insinuations that I hadn't done everything I might have done. Throughout Don's dying process I experienced forms of torture I didn't know existed. This was one.

For two years many people knew about Don's decline. It certainly wasn't a secret. We'd been open about it with our friends and folks at the hospital. As I walked to the snack bar one afternoon the human resources director stopped me. She was generally aware of what was going on. Kindly but bluntly she inquired about my emotional state and physical stamina given the level of responsibility I shouldered. She asked if I thought I could keep up the pace. I confessed to her that I felt tired and wasn't sleeping well. But I didn't say anything else. She nodded. While I appreciated the chat, I hadn't forgotten her professional position. Certainly she demonstrated concern for me as a human being in the midst of a very great, unwanted challenge, but she wouldn't have been doing her job if she hadn't been curious about my employment intentions down the line. Our brief exchange left me unsettled.

That was the first time the term *leave of absence* crossed my mind. Four months later it popped up again. I'd scheduled a meeting with one of the HR staff to learn more details about a multiple-month leave. I found out that the hospital would continue to carry Don and me on its group health insurance plan as long as we paid the premiums. Though it seemed like a fair arrangement, I doubted that we could afford those costs. Perhaps reading my face, the staffer back-pedaled a bit and assured me they would not insist upon the payments if we legitimately couldn't handle them. I wondered if she offered this because Don had given the hospital thousands of volunteer hours not long before. Regardless, I found myself thinking more about the benefits of a leave of absence over the next few weeks.

I talked about this possibility with several trusted friends, my priest, hospice personnel, and Don. Although these conversations began logically, they quickly became emotional. Opinions varied. Several folks reminded me that because my husband's life was limited, I would best serve him and us by retreating from work. I weighed the big risk associated with that choice: If Don outlived the leave period defined by hospital policy, I would have no job. We had minimal savings. Other people expressed the belief that my job provided a temporary escape from the harsh reality at home. One friend told me that while she loved Don and thought I should do whatever I could for him within reason, she didn't think I owed him my future financial security. The hospice director and one of her nurses questioned a leave's value in the fall of 1986; however, they had no idea when such action would be appropriate. The diversity of views compounded my confusion. It was like walking on a deserted road at midnight.

In February of 1987 Don openly displayed anger about my continuing to work. On one occasion he actually shouted, a rare outburst for him. For me, the dilemma was a matter of conscience. I had to listen to my conscience and decipher its message. I felt like my head was in a vice. Around this time a close friend counseled that all of this was a matter of the heart and I'd be wise to follow my heart. Pondering her words, I realized that I wasn't used to following my heart. I didn't trust it. I trusted my head. In the end logic won. I decided against the leave. The amputation of Don's leg a couple of weeks later might have made it necessary to choose differently. Either I would have been forced to take a leave of absence to care for him or I would have needed to admit him to a skilled nursing facility. With a newly amputated limb and a risk of more infection, he could not have remained in our apartment alone while I went to work.

Ever since the seriousness of Don's health situation had escalated, I'd been unsure about how much information to reveal to my boss and colleagues. I didn't want folks to doubt my ability to perform my duties, and I didn't want them to drive me crazy inquiring about Don's status every day. For those reasons I merely communicated a few basic facts until things reached the point where I had to say more. Of course holding our nightmare close to my chest deprived me of receiving empathy from people who might have been glad to offer it had they known more of the truth. Further, it denied them an opportunity to do something they might have needed to do. That was the trade-off. A coworker cornered me one day at the wall files and, in a low voice, said she'd recently heard about Don. She wanted to know if the rumor was true. I told her it was. Looking sad, she declared that she couldn't fathom how I coped with such a devastating prognosis. She implied that *she* couldn't. Tears bubbled up in her eyes. I thanked her for caring.

From the time Don lost his vision in 1980 we deliberated over how much to tell other people. Early on we discovered that most couldn't handle the whole truth—especially in a single dose. As a result, we volunteered distressing details incrementally. Folks needed time to digest what we'd told them the previous week or month before we added something new. Several close friends disappeared for a while. That really bothered Don; he felt rejected and unloved. It bothered me, too, but I accepted the behavior because I read the reasons fueling it: the not knowing what to say, the denial, the fear of death. All but one person eventually came around.

In addition we encountered folks who didn't grasp the severity of juvenile diabetes. In the hospital environment I heard educated (non-medical) people say that diabetes—regardless of type—wasn't a cancer diagnosis. According to them, we didn't need to worry much about it in the whole scheme of things. They didn't understand the unpredictability of the disease. Their perception was that if people with diabetes took insulin shots and avoided sweets, everything would be okay. I bristled. Ignorance about the disease seemed to be widespread. Ignorance about juvenile diabetes, in particular, is common. Perhaps that is the case because people with diabetes don't typically show signs of their disease. People resent somebody poking holes in their fantasies. Yet sometimes I did just that to set the record straight. I'd learned a great deal from reading medical textbooks as well as hearing patient stories. I provided education respectfully when ripe opportunities arose. It wasn't always welcomed.

Occasionally our knowledge worked against us with Don's doctors. Although we knew a lot about the disease progression, we weren't physicians. As licensed professionals on the case, they aimed to call the shots. They conducted examinations, ordered lab tests, and determined next moves. They didn't want our input. And they didn't want us to know that they disagreed among themselves on approach or that they lacked clarity about best actions to take. That was scary, but it was okay. We'd gotten to the point where the hat held no more rabbits.

A few months prior to his death Don shocked badly after eating a big meal. This didn't make sense. If anything, his blood sugar should have been high rather than low. I called the doctor to report the episode, my hands shaking. After a few moments of awkward silence followed by a sigh, he told me he didn't know what I should do. His parting words burned in my ears: "You've lived with this for a long time. Do what you think is best." Then he hung up. I felt abandoned and insecure. Did that mean I should give Don even more food? Or did it mean I should reduce the amount of insulin I injected the following morning? There were serious consequences to both. Neither of these options seemed intuitively efficacious.

A week before Don died one of the specialists making rounds in the critical care unit asked him if his wife clearly understood the meaning of not calling a code if his heart stopped. Don interpreted his tone as critical of his conscious decision against resuscitation. He assured this man that I supported these instructions. The doctor didn't drop the issue. Instead he recommended that Don reconsider. Exasperated, Don asked him why, as a terminally ill patient, he should do that, and explained that reviving him would only prolong his suffering. The doctor never replied.

Managing relationships with different specialist physicians with diverse personalities required energy, forethought, and finesse. Don didn't have extra energy to give; even if he had, he wouldn't have opted to expend it that way. Thus I assumed the role of mediator between my husband and the medical team. I did it for years. Don spoke with his doctors, but often angrily. Frequently he felt as if he wasn't being heard. More often than not he believed his questions were dismissed or answered incompletely. Immature arrogance and reluctance to discuss his impending death added fuel to the fire. Underneath everything else he harbored a simmering rage that stemmed from the fact that he hadn't yet died, despite acceptance of his fate. The doctors grew to dislike him.

I saw evidence of this in their body language and the facial expressions they worked hard to mask during visits. While Don couldn't see it, he sensed it. The two of us discussed it.

During hospital stays we quickly discovered that most nurses didn't fully comprehend diabetes. Although they administered Don's insulin shots, they generally didn't give them in a timely manner. This procedural snag usually resulted in unnecessary elevated blood glucose levels if he'd already eaten a meal. The reverse order created problems, too. Don went into shock if his body absorbed the insulin too far in advance of eating food. On several occasions I received calls at my office either from Don himself or nursing staff informing me of a crisis. This situation, unfortunately repeated during each hospital admission, demanded my steady attention. I didn't want to offend staff by pointing out errors, yet in the interest of Don's safety they had to be told. Insulin shocks destroy brain cells. Fluctuating blood sugars hasten the destruction of bodily organs. Educating nurses wasn't technically my job, but I took it on.

Our dilemmas demanded analysis and careful scrutiny. Making decisions about the dilemmas we faced wasn't easy. In retrospect I didn't make perfect decisions in every situation, but I did the best I could with the information I had at the time.

Chapter 7

SERVING OTHERS

For weeks after Don died I sometimes lay in bed at night listening to the autobiographical cassette tapes he'd produced during his active dying process. Positioning the recorder tight against my ear, I treasured the sound of his voice. Hearing it helped with the grief. Occasionally I played these tapes while I cleaned the apartment or prepared meals. Although they served a personal purpose at the time, they had been created to serve others. I hadn't forgotten Don's wish.

About a month into widowhood I received a call from Fritz, the director of program development for the local public television station. He had been a friend of ours and admired Don for his convictions, persistence, and courage. He expressed interest in some of the tapes. He wanted to make arrangements to pick them up because he had a project in mind. Intrigued, I inquired about it. He then shared his plans to write a feature article about Don's blindness and our marriage for the station's regional magazine. Fritz had been a regular contributor to this publication. He told me he'd decided to write our story using an interview style. I detected his excitement, mixed with concern. Fritz wondered if his request was coming too soon. In a sensitive tone he said he didn't want to intensify my pain. To his amazement I informed him that I viewed this project as a perfect use for the tapes and that I would support his efforts in any way I could. He asked me to make notes that would aid him in organizing the voluminous material. Enthusiastically I agreed.

By the fall of 1987 Fritz had gotten permission from his employer to write the article. He'd devoted hours to going through the tapes and drafting an outline. However, he'd concluded that he needed my input to round out the story. We set a date. He and his wife invited me to their home in the country for dinner, and afterwards Fritz interviewed me into the night. Later he told me I'd offered some "really candid and lovely stuff."

The six-page article—including photos—was published in December. In terms of both content and integrity the finished product exceeded my expectations. I had trusted Fritz to tell the truth. He hadn't disappointed me. The piece aligned with Don's goal to educate the public about blindness as well as juvenile diabetes. What I didn't know was that it was only the first of two opportunities to accomplish this. I copied the article and sent it to family and friends as a Christmas gift.

That year had been difficult for me for obvious reasons. Don's long-term suffering had culminated in death, and I had become a widow. But something else happened that same year. It was big. One of my co-workers, Laverne, shockingly diagnosed with liver cancer the previous summer, finally died in June. As her health declined, she and I became friends. From the outset Don knew about her problems, and he sometimes went with me to visit her at home as long as he was able.

After she recovered from her initial hospitalization, Lavern continued to report for work in the business office. As long as she could function, she wanted to stay involved. She wanted to be around people. The blow of bad news along with the proposed rigorous chemotherapy regimen had thrown her off balance. Alone with me she confided that she was scared.

Lavern's presence unnerved most of the women in the office. They weren't comfortable with her falls on the floor, her foggy brain, her tears. I noticed many avoided her. Some talked behind her back, not unkindly but curiously. They questioned the department head's judgment when she allowed Lavern to resume her duties. Although I understood their reaction, I refused to let Lavern flounder alone. During breaks I sought her out and invited her to vent. She appreciated that.

In August of 1986 Lavern's doctors put her back in the hospital. One Sunday afternoon I visited, wearing my lavender dress and shoes, her favorite color. When I entered the room, I saw people literally lining the walls. They chatted among themselves but totally ignored the patient. How ironic. The noise level, inappropriate for the circumstances, annoyed me. A nurse was in the process of removing the morphine drip. I wondered why.

A couple of days later my question was answered. When I returned with a colleague who was also my friend, Lavern announced that chemotherapy had been scheduled to start very soon. It was expected to be a long bout. Though my lavender tea roses displayed on the window sill made her smile, they didn't erase the anxiety consuming the whole of her face. At the end of the visit Lavern grabbed my arm and begged me not to leave. She tried to hug me, her fingernails digging into the back of my neck. As I turned to go she asked about Don. Abruptly, then, she changed the topic to work. She complained bitterly that "the girls," as she called them, never visited. She wanted to see them. I explained that a few had stopped by when she'd been asleep. She squeezed her eyes shut, perhaps disbelieving. And it was true that many of the women with whom I worked refused to visit because they didn't know what to say. They worried about saying the wrong thing. They worried about awkward silence. It was better to stay away. Gently I told them that presence counted more than words. Some feared sick people, especially those lying in hospital beds. They disliked the sterility of wards, the antiseptic smells, the anxious whispers in halls. One voiced disgust for the chronically ill. By hiding at their desks my colleagues blotted out a reality they clearly resisted.

Others in Lavern's world resisted her reality, too. I personally heard a neighbor and a family member tell her how good she looked to them. They conducted their brief visits through a distorted lens that helped them cope. As they delivered these nonsensical messages, Lavern turned her head to the other side of her pillow. She didn't speak.

Deeper into her hospital stay Lavern became very depressed. Further, she was worn out from the treatment. For hours she lay without moving or showing signs of life. One of the oncology nurses urged her to join the hospital's cancer support group. She angrily rejected that suggestion, insisting she could cope. At the end of the month her doctor sent her home armed with plenty of morphine.

Chemo began again by Labor Day. Though rigorous, this time it was administered on an outpatient basis: once a week for three consecutive months. With the second round, Lavern lost her appetite and quite a bit of weight. When I saw her I thought she looked gaunt from nausea and fatigue. By the middle of September significant pain had set in. By phone Don counseled her to take her pills regularly, but she hated their negative effects. He then proposed an alternative medication recalled from his hospice volunteer days. Reluctantly she requested it, and her doctor prescribed it. For a while the substitute seemed to help.

To my surprise Lavern pretended everything was fine. I noticed in her a definite denial of the facts that relentlessly ruled her life. Our conversations centered on clothes, meals, vacations, and her hope of returning to work. She squelched any attempts to talk about what was really going on. Occasionally she spoke positively of the future.

By the middle of October she landed flat on her back. A brief hospital stay followed. Unfortunately a violent reaction to a powerful new drug had wrecked her fragile stability. Despite its devastating adverse consequences, her oncologist argued stridently to continue the regimen. Hearing her distress, I advised Lavern to take charge of her own life. It hadn't occurred to her to do that. She tearfully described the treatments as nasty. She wasn't sure she could endure them anymore. Yet she didn't stand up to the doctor. She chose not to exercise her rights. As a result she spent the Christmas season at home with a mouth full of sores and inflammation of other mucosal surfaces. Simply sitting in a chair hurt. The chemotherapy was burning her body.

The turning point came in January of 1987. A CT scan showed the cancer was winning. She had three choices: stop the chemo, pursue experimental procedures in a large city, or resume the current therapy. In a panic Lavern called me at home to talk. She needed to make a decision, and she had no idea how to do it. I gave her my time and attention, but Don was actively dying then. For the next two months I stayed focused mostly on him. Sometime that winter I learned that Lavern chose to continue treatment locally. Supposedly she'd said only a fool wouldn't do it. It was an aggressive, last-ditch effort to save her. If the therapy fizzled, she was going to die.

Deep inside I always knew the outcome. All odds were stacked against survival. Lavern died in June, exactly three months after Don. During those last weeks I visited often, both at her home and at the hospital. In April I observed her swollen face and legs, the slow drip of multiple IV medications, the food pump, and the ever-present morphine infuser. I was aware of her bloated belly, cramps, nausea, and fevers. I saw evidence of increasing systemic weakness, and I'd heard about periodic hallucinations. Without shame I advocated only for her comfort. Willingly I assisted nurses with ordinary tasks: lifting her up in bed in a blanket, feeding her ice chips or Jell-O from a spoon, positioning straws between her lips. On walks I pushed IV poles through the halls. Once, to help her relax and distract her, I massaged her arm as staff struggled off and on for hours to insert needles in a worn-out vein. It was tough to watch.

For me, it hurt to be on the hospital floors in general. Not long ago Don had suffered and died there, and I was still grieving. Soon my grief would be compounded with the passing of Lavern. After stroking her forehead for a while on Easter afternoon I stepped into the elevator and cried. From the beginning I'd made a commitment to be there even if it wasn't convenient, uplifting, or fun.

Throughout that year-long ordeal my colleagues and bosses had looked to me for direction and support. Because Lavern repeatedly told me how much she missed her friends, I urged them to go to her. When a few admitted they couldn't do it alone, I invited them to come along with me. One woman said she felt better with a buddy. Eventually this same woman followed my lead and held Lavern's hand, a demonstration of care and concern she'd previously avoided. Later she told me she found strength in me. Progress was slow. But when two cowering co-workers delivered a bouquet of tulips to Lavern's hospital room in April, I knew things were turning around.

Senior leaders in my department, however, carefully kept their distance. One commented that my ability to continue walking into her room day after day exhibited a courage that far exceeded his. The department head herself relied on me to provide status reports when she phoned. This woman unequivocally respected what I was doing and apologized for avoiding Lavern in her compromised condition. I marveled how I, having no recognized authority in that office, served as her chief source of information. After Lavern died, my direct supervisor remarked that Don would have been pleased and proud if he'd known that unlike her I had stayed with Lavern through thick and thin. I nodded.

It wasn't easy for me to stay. It wasn't easy for Roy, her husband, either. From the time she'd received her cancer diagnosis he lost weight. Over the course of that awful year he shed forty pounds. His clothes hung on his skinny frame like bags, his pant legs covering the tops of his shoes. His wrists were so thin his watch fell off. The bones in his face were pronounced. I used to study him as he slept in the hospital room chair and thought he resembled a scarecrow. I observed the fatigue, tension, and fear in him that never went away. Seeing it brought back painful memories.

For months Roy chose to remain in the background during my visits. As he watched me closely while I talked with his wife, I wasn't sure what he was thinking. His discomfort with dying was obvious. Two months before her death he joked about her macabre physical appearance, perhaps to stay sane. Other times he attempted mild humor that irked Lavern. Sometimes he tried to force her to eat. He told her yogurt would make her strong. When she pushed the spoon away, he sucked in his breath. All of his movements screamed frustration and annoyance. Roy didn't understand that between the cancer and the treatment, she had no interest in food. He didn't grasp that ultimately food possessed no power to heal her. Once his tension appeared so great that I wondered if he might smash something right there in our midst. I could relate.

In retrospect, Roy loved her as best he could. He brought her fresh flowers on a regular basis, usually lavender roses or an orchid. He spoke to her softly using words of affection. He stayed long hours by her bedside. Despite working a swing shift, he managed to keep it up. Although I saw all of this, I also witnessed his denial. In mid-May, three weeks before she died, I initiated a touchy conversation with him outside her room, hoping he would open up to me. I told him Lavern was worried about him and their son and what her disease was doing to them. Roy looked uncomfortable, but he let me finish. Then, turning on his heels, he nervously proceeded to tell me that he'd baked a cake all by himself because he'd been hungry for one all week. That was his way of shutting me down.

Lavern got sick all over the bed just as we walked back into the room. Shaking his head, Roy said he couldn't figure out why such a thing happened. The bed sheets had been changed earlier; now they had to be changed again. For months Lavern had confided that Roy hadn't accepted her illness. He desperately wanted to believe that she would get well and go home. He cried and told her he needed her. He refused to discuss any of it. The wall between them grew.

Four days before the end Lavern informed her husband that she wasn't going to live. She did it more boldly than I ever would have imagined. She said she didn't want to die and was afraid. Roy begged her not to say those things, and asked what would happen to him when she was gone. She assured him he could live without her; that he didn't need her anymore. Big tears slid down his hollow cheeks.

I learned in confidence from a ward clerk that Lavern's doctors had decided a long time ago that Lavern and Roy couldn't handle the fact of her dying and had made the decision to lie, in essence, about the seriousness of her condition. One actually told Lavern somewhere along the way that her cancer was treatable. I cringed when I heard that. Perhaps if physicians had been honest earlier in the game, Lavern and Roy would have reached a place where they could have talked a bit more openly about her poor prognosis and impending death. I believed they'd been cheated. It made me sad.

The morning after she died Roy called me at home. His voice cracked as he gave me the news. Suddenly he found himself in the position of having to face what he'd held at bay for so long. I was gentle with him. The next day Lavern's son phoned. At twenty-eight he'd not yet experienced death and grief. It all felt strange to him. He said his chest hurt and he hadn't cried. He kept insisting he had to be strong for his father. A couple of days later at the funeral home I handed him a little piece of paper. On it I'd written, "Even dying can work for the good. I have found this to be true."

The next week Roy came to our business office to clean out Lavern's desk. He seemed reasonably cheerful and in control. Someone had offered to box the items and deliver them to his house, but he insisted on doing the job himself. I thought he might have wanted to see the girls one last time.

On a July evening he called me to chat. I of all people understood that need. Trying to muster the energy, I sat still in a chair and listened. Roy reported that he'd sorted through Lavern's personal belongings, that he'd cleaned up the yard, and that he'd taken a big bike ride with his son. As he wound down, he expressed regret over Lavern dying in the hospital instead of at home as she'd wished. He told me he didn't know how he'd have handled it himself if she'd have spent her final weeks in their bed. Prior to her last hospital stay he'd done twenty-one loads of laundry every seven days and only slept two hours a night. It was brutal. I assured him that Lavern had benefitted from excellent inpatient nursing care when the signs of dying escalated. Being at home with her complications might not have worked. He agreed.

Chapter 8

ACCEPTING CHANGE

When I stopped to think about it, I realized Roy and I walked a similar path. As a widower and widow, both of us faced a point of crisis and massive change we hadn't chosen. Sometimes we resented it; other times we embraced it. Our reaction depended on the events of the day. At the core, though, the way he and I dealt with loss differed. Roy worked to exhaustion to numb his pain; I allowed myself to feel it. And I didn't want to waste it. In one of her diaries Anne Morrow Lindbergh wrote that she believed women absorb and conquer sorrow differently from men. Women, she said, take it willingly and blend it into the fiber of their lives. They build something from it and with it.

A couple of weeks after Don's death in March I'd stood at my front storm door and stared unseeingly across the street. My stomach in knots, I was sharply aware of a huge hole in my life I didn't know how to fill. Then, I still had Lavern. In a strange way that comforted me. When she died in June, I stood in the same place behind the screen, wondering what my future held. My two big jobs were done. After a Sunday concert at my college alma mater not long afterwards I met one of my mother's former teaching colleagues while walking out of the music building. With noticeable emotion she offered her condolences. "I'm a thirty-three-year-old widow," I told her. "What am I to do with that?" She paused, looked deeply into my eyes, and said, "A lot."

Empty hand syndrome was a kind of desert. No longer was I actively involved with taking care of other people. The caretaking, though demanding and tedious, had provided a clear focus. Now I didn't know what to do with the blank slate. The void made me nervous.

One night I dreamed of Don. In this dream he'd returned to me for only a few days. We sailed happily to an unnamed island. The details of our activities there were nebulous. At the end of the allotted time together, he boarded a ship alone. He instructed me to remain on the island. Back home I received a brief note from him. He simply wrote "I love you" in a foreign language. Upon waking I pondered possibilities for the dream's meaning. The one I settled on was this: Youthful and alive, I was not to follow Don in death. There was something more for me. I was to create a new life.

Another dream reassured me that I didn't need to worry about him. Don was lying in the hospital, and doctors had predicted that he would die within minutes. All life-sustaining equipment had been removed. A few people lined the sides of the bed with me, watching and waiting for the final breath. Suddenly, to everyone's shock, Don sat up, got out of bed, and walked unaided across the room. Several nurses tried to put him back into the bed, but he continued to rise. In this dream he never died. As I woke up, I saw him walking into the hall as if to leave us.

After a women's group meeting one evening a friend of mine tapped my arm in the parking lot on the way to our cars. She told me she thought I looked good physically despite everything that had happened. We talked for a little while before she said, "Don died when he knew you were prepared to let him go and take care of yourself. He wanted to be sure you could stand on your own two feet without him. He held on for you." Her eyes bored into mine. I never forgot her words.

According to many folks around me, my body didn't show obvious signs of having walked through a scorching fire. Though pencil-thin, with a pancake face, I'd stayed reasonably healthy during those last two years. I'd caught a few head colds, but nothing worse. Actually, it was amazing given the ongoing insomnia and stress. But significant weight loss had altered my heart rhythm. During a routine visit one of my doctors threatened to admit me to the hospital if I lost one more pound. I started to drink high-calorie milkshakes hoping to hold the scales steady. Who would care for Don if I wasn't there?

Those rhythm changes were potentially dangerous. A generic cardiac problem had been detected in my twenties, the year following my mother's unexpected death. Medical technology in the 1970s was not advanced enough to nail a specific diagnosis, but sophisticated electrocardiography during a crisis many years later revealed a condition called supraventricular tachycardia (SVT). While I didn't know the precise nature of my heart issues while Don was dying, intuitively I knew to exercise caution; losing too much weight disturbed cardiac function.

As a new widow I experienced unsettling—even frightening—heart rate and heart rhythm irregularities from time to time. A few landed me in the emergency room where doctors converted an abnormal sinus rhythm to normal. My cardiologists varied the dosages of different drugs, never quite finding the magic bullet. Once I was unstable for months, my heart rate so rapid I barely performed activities of daily living without scrupulous concern. At night I lay rigid in bed, my heart pounding in my ears like a hammer on wood. It took hours to fall asleep. Most likely the hormonal fluctuations in my thirties as well as the uncertainties of widowhood aggravated the situation.

I had read somewhere that all change is good. In that first year alone I wasn't sure. Many familiar relationships had shifted subtly into something that didn't feel comfortable to me. I tried to figure out what had caused the shift. Books written by other widows helped me figure it out. For nearly eight years I'd been part of a couple; now I was single. People didn't know how to relate to Sylvia in her new role. They also didn't know who I had become as a result of the suffering and death. It seemed we all had sea legs.

At work my boss timidly asked how I was doing. She sought the truth. I told her I was glad to be busy, free of serious distractions on the home front. I frequently caught colleagues watching me out of the corners of their eyes. Their glances betrayed their assessments of the extent of the supposed damage. Understandably they wondered if I was fragile. Until then I'd never regarded myself as particularly brittle or weak, but in the early months without Don those words might have applied. Occasionally I felt like an egg with a hairline crack in it. If someone looked at me crosswise or inquired how I was getting along, I feared I might break wide open. I was vulnerable in a new way. This vulnerability was real and raw and sad. For most of my life people had viewed me as a strong person. But I didn't feel strong. I just looked that way on the outside to others. My emotions didn't match the image I projected.

A man who had observed me from afar for months stopped me on a downtown sidewalk and said he wouldn't have believed I'd been recently widowed if he didn't know the fact of it. He continued to tell me that whenever he'd seen me, I appeared to be confident and in control. The hospice director used to remark that I seemed to be perfectly together. A woman from Don's INSIGHT group told me I always impressed her as calm and cool. Another observed that in public I'd kept on smiling even during the worst of the grief. It was true; I smiled often. But I smiled to push back the tears that bubbled just beneath the surface.

A much older and wiser Southern friend, Sheldon Vanauken (Van), with whom I enjoyed regular correspondence for a period of years, wrote that I'd been tested and was now stronger than I realized. He knew the core of me. I tried to trust his assessment. In a subsequent note he observed that I seemed to be doing well psychologically according to the content of my letters. He saw no red flags. Because of his own intense experience with grief after the death of his young wife, and the accounts that hundreds of grieving people had shared with him over two decades after the release of his award-winning book about that experience, I viewed him as a credible gauge for progress. I began to consider that perhaps it was possible to *feel* weak but in reality be strong. This valued mentor got me thinking that feelings were not necessarily accurate indicators of truth.

I felt emotionally safe with Van. We had a platonic but solid history. I believed he wouldn't hurt me. But I didn't have that same assurance about men I didn't know. I found their stares and words disconcerting. To them I was an available woman, no longer married and no longer tied down. Perceiving no barrier, a few invited me to dinner. In those early months I wasn't ready for dates. I was stuck somewhere between the past and the present, in a place without a name. I had nothing to give to men. An exception was Roy, with whom I shared the common thread of Lavern. He insisted on thanking me for my faithfulness to his wife in her suffering. I agreed to dine with him only if he understood that I was consenting to do it as a friend. My sense was that he hoped for more, but he agreed to my terms. We went to a restaurant once and spoke a little by phone for a while after that.

My married friends' husbands made themselves more visible to me when I visited their homes. Their faces showed signs of pleasure when they answered the door to find me standing there in bright sunlight or soft lamplight on their porches. No one crossed a line, but I noticed a distinct difference in their behavior. Before Don's death they tended to be quiet, disinterested, remote. It was as if they'd merely tolerated or accepted my presence. Now they initiated conversations and expected me to participate in animated discussions about a myriad of topics. They'd come out of hiding. Not wanting to jeopardize my long-standing relationships with their wives, I became leery in their company.

Once I baked an apple pie and delivered it to a close friend. I knew that everyone in her family loved it, and I was pleased to present my gift. As soon as her husband spied the pie, he embarrassed me and her with his extended lavish praise. Unfortunately it didn't stop there. He went on to say that his wife's talents with pastry fell far short of mine. I wanted to drop through the floor. This sort of thing would not have happened when Don was alive.

Holidays were especially hard. I felt like a displaced person. It seemed like I didn't belong anywhere. Occasionally my three single, adopted aunts insisted that I join them if they were available. But most of the people in my life had partners and children. Easter came first after Don's death, and I decided to invite one of my sisters and her family for the weekend. We enjoyed a good time together. I laughed when my three-year-old niece stuck her nose into fragrant bulb flowers, and snapped photos as she hunted her basket of eggs and candy. Those couple of days gave me a taste of normalcy. After the family left to return to New York, I went to the hospital to visit Lavern.

While driving in the car I sometimes thought about how Don's death differed from my mother's and how the two events had affected me. My mother had died catastrophically in an instant when a heart catheterization had gone terribly wrong; Don had died slowly as diabetes ravaged his organs. Both deaths turned my world upside down. My mother had been the center of the home when I and my siblings were growing up. In some ways Don had been the head of our home after I married him. Immediately following both deaths I questioned my ability to recover. But losing my mother had taught me resilience; that was the silver lining in the calamity. Thus after Don's death I didn't so much question my ability to survive but rather my capacity to create a new life on my own. I had no idea how I was going to do that. Feeling rather insecure, I saw the world as an unpredictable place.

Both deaths had changed my financial picture as well as my world view. Prior to her death my mother had promised to help chisel away at my sizable and burdensome college loans. This, of course, never happened. She didn't live long enough to make a contribution. As a result I spent the greater part of a decade paying off my undergraduate education. Upon Don's death his Social Security Disability checks came to a halt, reducing my monthly income. I received a tiny one-time death benefit; that was it. In the fall our landlord had raised the rent. While Don was alive that hadn't presented a significant problem, but it did then. Suddenly I found myself robbing Peter to pay Paul in order to cover the monthly expenses with the minimal compensation I earned from my job at the hospital. Things definitely got tougher financially.

It didn't help that everyone around me seemed to be clueless about young widows. People associated widowhood with women over sixty. Nobody knew what to do with me. While I had contemplated what life as an individual might be like as Don was dying, I had not considered how I would fit—or not fit—into organizations and my social network. Naïvely I'd assumed that folks would accept me as they had before, and that the path would be made clear. I was wrong. My experience of widowhood was more like trying to stand upright on a moving floor. About two months into it I opted to attend my fifteenth high school class reunion at a local country club. When I arrived I noticed I was the only person there without a partner. Classmates treated me kindly, but conversation was sparse.

Not long after that event I committed to reevaluating my perceptions and understandings of the world. It was important for me to identify which of them no longer applied. I also knew I needed to reassess my beliefs and attitudes toward change. This involved an examination of the mental messaging that played minute by minute in my head. Over several months this proved to be an eye-opening exercise that gradually led to several critical revisions. The most profound discovery? I could alter the story I'd been telling myself about *change*. I could manage change instead of allowing change to manage me. I could take charge of my circumstances rather than let them determine the content and quality of my life. That powerful realization directed my future.

Other useful realizations quickly followed. On a conscious level I saw that I could decide to welcome the changes that had landed in my lap without excessive anger or fear. I determined that change didn't have to be bad. In my family of origin change had been viewed as something to reject automatically no matter what it was. My widowhood presented an opportunity to see it differently. Now I understood that I could neutralize change and simply see it as my reality. Learning to adapt came easier that way. I knew I'd progressed when I realized that change didn't have to hurt more than anything else I'd experienced. Making peace with change was a choice.

In one of her books Marianne Williamson stated that every change is a challenge to become who we really are. Assuming that is true, then Don's death was to play a significant role in my evolution as a human being. In fact, perhaps it was meant to be the catalyst in a major evolution. The changes I faced invited me to pay attention to possibility and opportunity. They dared me to reframe my loss to both myself and others. How could my loss and the changes it brought position me for something bigger, deeper, and better going forward? I thought about things like this generically in 1987, but I wasn't ready to act.

I also came to believe that navigating the waves of change required some effort on my part. I had to map out a basic coping course that was right for me, then steer the ship through both calm and rough waters. I'd never been a person to float. As a firstborn I was a do-er who took responsibility for my life. Although I didn't need to have all the answers, I needed to have ideas about how I'd get through each day.

The longer I walked through widowhood, the more I became aware of hidden gifts in the change I was living. I had time to spend with friends, became interested in redecorating some rooms in my apartment, and had energy to travel. Abandoning a rigid schedule, I could eat when I wanted to eat, watch late night movies, and read books in bed on rainy Saturday mornings. I signed up for painting classes and later voice lessons. No one depended on me—at least not in the way Don had depended on me hour by hour. Sometimes the freedom surprised me.

Chapter 9

FACING TRUTH

With that freedom came responsibility. I fully grasped this truth. Further, I felt both a strong desire and an obligation to use what I'd learned during my marriage—self-control, endurance, patience, trust in the process of life, greater sensitivity to suffering, and practical strategies for caring for the sick—to serve other people. Without a doubt I'd had to face several very hard facts when Don was losing his vision and later when he was dying. These included realizing our lives would be altered forever; knowing that I was going to have to do some difficult, unpleasant things; accepting that I couldn't save him; and reconciling that eventually I would be left alone. By meeting those facts head-on and living them day to day, I grew as a person in ways I couldn't have imagined. I wanted to leverage that growth and education—not waste it.

Within a week of Don's death a young registered nurse who was aware of my situation approached me on the sidewalk at the hospital. She had recently spoken privately to me of her own grief related to losing her boyfriend nine months previously. She didn't know quite what to say after inquiring how I was getting along. I filled the momentary silence with an invitation to supper. Accepting it, she smiled and told me she imagined I might be able to help her. As I turned away, I acknowledged being curious about how she thought a wet-behind-the-ears widow could do that. But she must have sensed something.

Perhaps the most startling truth I had to confront was the crushing certainty of Don's *deathness*—his physical presence gone from my living space, his never coming back. I didn't disturb his clothes in the bureau drawers and closet for several months before I finally mustered the courage to list most of them with a consignment shop. The finality associated with boxing up his familiar pants, shirts, jackets, and sweaters one late spring afternoon almost brought me to tears. Still, I didn't cry. I kept on sorting and packing. In the end I saved three favorite items with which I could not bring myself to part.

As I dealt with the clothing, I recalled a recent dream in which Don had asked me to drive him to a pub. In the dream he stayed at the pub until I came by several hours later. He was wearing his navy V-neck sweater and a white shirt, a combination I liked. We sat close together at the table and talked. I was surprised when he told me that despite his blindness he'd gone walking for two miles while I'd been gone. He proceeded to assure me that his lack of vision didn't matter because he was physically healthy in every other way. When I thought about it, I regarded the dream as a gift because I'd had trouble remembering Don with stable health ever since his death.

Something else of significance happened around that same time. For at least a year my friend Van and a literary acquaintance of his had known of my desire to become a published nonfiction author. After some discussion they invited me to write a lengthy personal essay for possible inclusion in a book project Van's acquaintance had coordinated. Upon reading it they pronounced my piece moving and powerful. Because of their positive response I naturally assumed that my essay would be part of the book. Months later, however, I was informed that it had not been selected in the final analysis. When I notified Van he was shocked. In my letter to him I conveyed my disappointment and frustration. Immediately he approached his acquaintance about considering me for other avenues.

Within weeks one came unexpectedly in a phone call from the editor of a family magazine in Boston. She had contacted me upon recommendation from Van's acquaintance and because she had read my essay, which he had forwarded to her. She said she saw evidence of my writing skill and potential. At the end of our conversation she asked me to do a feature article for their December issue about how to cope with Christmas after a loved one dies. If my work was accepted unanimously for publication by the review board, I would be offered additional opportunities with their magazine. When I hung up I was elated. Just as the old saying goes, another door opened when the first door closed.

That was the beginning of a five-year paid writing commitment I hadn't expected. Excited and inspired, I decided to convert the nondescript spare bedroom in my apartment into a study complete with a big desk, a state-of-the-art typewriter, and a comfortable reading chair. I chose a fresh color scheme, took down the dark blinds, and hung new curtains. My redecorating efforts shifted the energy in that space. Satisfied with the changes, I felt ready to spend countless evening and weekend hours in that little room doing work I loved.

By the fall of 1987 five of my feature articles on various topics had been published, and more were planned. Initially my writing was based on deeply personal experiences such as Don's blindness, his dying process, and my widowhood. But soon my editor probed my interest in researching selected community and social issues. One of them was life in jail from the perspective of the incarcerated. Never having visited a prison, I jumped at the chance to go behind the walls and interview inmates.

A year later I was receiving letters about my articles from reader fans, including state prison inmates, forwarded to my home address by magazine office staff. I personally responded to every note and letter. I figured that if people took the time to write to me, the least I could do was honor their efforts. In a few cases friendships grew as a result of the correspondence. With inmates, however, I remained guarded. When I discussed this with the city police chief he cautioned me about appearing to encourage relationships with these men. I described their lengthy, often detailed, extremely friendly letters. Surely viewing me as naïve, he told me he didn't want to see problems develop. Inmates, starved for companionship and affection, might misinterpret my motives and assume I wanted something more than a casual connection. He suggested that I open a post office box to collect this mail and limit the number of letters to each man living in a correctional facility. It was wise advice.

Eventually I needed to face the truth: Most male inmates who were initially interested in my article content soon became more interested in me as a woman. My photograph was typically published at the end of my articles along with a little blurb about me. A number of them commented on it. A few told me they had torn it off the page and kept it in their cell. This raised a red flag. One began to write blatantly disparaging remarks about Don after he decided he'd fallen in love with me. He was angry because I didn't return his feelings. Before things got out of hand I decided to stop writing to all inmates except one. The man with whom I maintained contact for several years understood the boundaries.

The fifth anniversary celebration of the blind support group Don had founded in 1982 took place that fall. On a beautiful, warm Friday evening I attended a home-style dinner recognizing this milestone at a local restaurant. One of the long-standing INSIGHT members had baked a fancy chocolate cake with a congratulations message in frosting on top. I sat next to a Lions Club representative, another invited guest. While folks at my table ate and talked, another truth became obvious to me: Life goes on, and things evolve. Clearly Don was absent from the event, and this group had matured. Anita, the woman who had replaced Don as coordinator and facilitator, had done a good job. She admitted that she wasn't a natural leader at the time she assumed the role, but she succeeded in making progress. I was happy for her.

After the meal Anita stood at the podium and introduced me before I delivered a brief speech. I'd planned my message carefully, as I wanted Don to be proud if he could hear it. I began by thanking folks for their monetary contributions to the National Federation of the Blind in my husband's memory. Then I reminded them of the purpose of the group and said that it had been formed in love. I conveyed my interest in its survival and well-being. I offered my continued friendship. In closing I told them that INSIGHT was never Don's group—it was their group. It was his gift to them. I challenged each and every person to nurture it and use it wisely.

At the end of the evening a member of the support group tugged at my sleeve. She thanked me for my remarks, then asked me if I was dating. Her sudden, direct inquiry caught me by surprise. Feeling a desire to escape, I muttered that I hadn't met anyone yet and quickly extricated myself from the venue. Driving home I reflected on my femininity and sexuality and how, because of circumstances, it essentially had been lying dormant for years. This was a painful thought. I knew that to some folks' way of thinking, I had sacrificed much of my youth to care for a blind, chronically ill husband who had died.

In April of 1988 the Lebanon Lions Club held a press conference. With great enthusiasm they formally announced that in partnership with the local public television station they planned to produce a sixty-minute documentary to improve the sighted public's understanding of the blind. Three years before Don had challenged the club to take on such a project. His goal was to cut through some of the ignorance, prejudice, and fear that abounded. He wanted the film to tell the truth about what it was like to live blind. It appeared that his dream would be realized. When the Lions Club first approached the television station, the idea was welcomed. Our friend, Fritz, had assumed responsibility for conducting the research to determine the need. The results confirmed Don's suspicions: not much material existed on this topic.

Kicking off such a major project depended on locating funds to support it. Both the Lions Club and the television station estimated that production of the video and an accompanying satellite teleconference would cost $75,000. Although the president of Lions International reviewed the proposal and showed interest in it, he told the Lebanon organization that they had to find the money by themselves. A key staffer at the Lebanon Community Library helped the Lions obtain a grant, and a local foundation promised to provide $60,000 of the total cost if the Lions Club supplied the remaining $15,000.

As an honored guest, I attended the Lions Club luncheon event during which the project was unveiled. I was seated next to the INSIGHT support group coordinator at a table that included the city mayor, several Lions Club members, and a person Don had known who was blind. It pleased me to see evidence of my late husband's recommendations being taken seriously on such a wide scale. The truth was that despite past differences, the Lions respected Don's judgment.

After the meal a newspaper reporter interviewed me privately in an adjacent room. She intended to capture my reaction to the grant and the upcoming project at large. She also invited me to comment on what I believed would have been Don's response if he had lived to share the excitement. The printed article in the paper the next day quoted me as having said that Don would have been very pleased but that he'd also have felt some anxiety due to the enormity of the challenge. Further, that I was committed to ongoing active involvement with the project, specifically as a consultant to video production and a member of the film's advisory board. I stated that Don would have served in these capacities, and it was my privilege to do so in his absence.

As I prepared to leave the press conference, I thanked key people for inviting me to the event. The previous Lions president shook my hand and laughed. He told me that the last time he'd looked down on me from a head table was at the Lions board meeting when Don presented his concerns about the white cane fundraiser. Both of us certainly remembered that tense, unpleasant evening. Smiling broadly, I replied that thankfully this was a much happier occasion for everyone.

Fritz wrote the script for the video and landed the job as producer after another producer originally assigned to the project resigned. In the fall of 1988 he contacted me to discuss his plans for using some of the material in Don's tapes as well as for interviewing me and selected others on camera soon. Fritz envisioned filming me in four action scenes which would serve as backdrops for various segments of the interview.

At the beginning of November Fritz and the film director showed up at my office to get the key to my apartment. They needed a few hours to set up filming equipment before I got home. A flood of brilliant white light shone through the living room curtains as I pulled into the driveway, my heart pounding. Two grinning men greeted me behind the door. Immediately I noticed they had moved all the furniture. The director suggested that I dull the color on my cheeks with additional face powder. He cautioned that the camera could be harsh. As soon as I freshened up in the bathroom, we got to work.

We spent thirty minutes on the first scene: me walking into a dark house, switching on the lights, sorting through mail, and hanging up my coat. Fritz rehearsed the scene with me and laid out the sequence before we began shooting. It was interesting to discover that I wasn't particularly nervous. I tried to flow with what they asked me to do.

The second scene involved me cooking supper. The director filmed the entire process, including me eating part of the meal. The final segment at my apartment consisted of Fritz interviewing me on the sofa. I was encouraged when both men told me that I had performed better than some professionals. During a partial replay of the video stream I saw for myself that I appeared relaxed and natural. Actually, I'd found it fun. But three hours in front of a camera was exhausting.

We shot the final scene in a nearby restaurant four months later. When I arrived the TV crew and a stand-in Don were waiting in the dining room. I caught my breath as I stared at the man chosen to play the role of my husband. The physical likeness was slightly unnerving. Before filming could begin I had to teach this actor how to use a white cane, take my arm, and eat a meal as a blind man would eat. At one point during our practice runs he told me he worried about how seeing him would affect me emotionally. I told him that the experience, though strange, didn't upset me. Lunch proved to be stimulating between the stress involved with filming and several Lions Club leaders serving as fellow diners.

Back home we filmed additional clips that focused on objects in the living room and another couple pretending to visit. Snow was falling hard by the time we wrapped up the final scene in the freezing outdoors. Fritz promised that I'd get to view the finished product prior to its debut to the full Lions Club membership.

This opportunity came in May. One evening Fritz and his wife stopped by my apartment. For thirty minutes we watched in silence. Afterwards I offered feedback and thanked Fritz for his professionalism and diligent efforts. Expressing relief that the project was finished, he admitted to fatigue, complacency, and boredom after working and reworking the material over and over again. He also lamented the fact that he'd identified a few technical disappointments. Fine-tuned equipment that had been unavailable to the crew might have prevented them. I told him I doubted that the average viewer possessed the skill to detect those sorts of details. As he walked out the door, he assured me that I'd receive my own copy of the tape within a few short weeks.

Eleven months later the completed documentary entitled *Living Blind* aired on public television. In a newspaper interview a Lions Club past president stated that the film would dispel myths about blind people's abilities. He said blind people are not horribly handicapped unless they choose to be. Club members who viewed the film sat spellbound as they watched it for the first time. The newspaper article that captured highlights from this interview also discussed the proposed teleconference in which Lions Clubs across the country would participate after viewing the film simultaneously. A toll-free number was to be provided, allowing members to ask their questions directly to a panel of Lions, people who were blind, and others associated with vision loss.

My involvement with this project inspired me to do more with my personal experiences. I wanted to impact other people's lives deeply. I wanted to play big. I just didn't know what *big* looked like then.

Chapter 10

SPREADING MY WINGS

I felt restless, ready to move, eager to create and build. In my diary I'd made a note to the effect that I felt like I was wasting away in a dark corner of the world and that I had so much to give but nowhere to give it. I yearned to spread my wings. The answers I sought weren't coming fast enough. I was impatient.

One night I dreamed of trying to find a familiar highway on foot. For what seemed like hours I wandered around hoping to spot signs pointing me in the right direction. For a while I walked in circles. All of a sudden I looked up and saw the road stretched out like white ribbon before me. Relieved and satisfied, I immediately woke up. That dream signified my search for whatever was meant to come next in my life. It also prompted me to watch for signs. It gave me hope.

As I skimmed the newspaper one summer day in 1988, I accidentally spied a sizable help-wanted ad for an office manager at the hospital's brand-new kidney dialysis center. I'd been aware of the center while it was under construction, and I was interested in the service it was designed to provide. Don had not been a viable candidate for kidney dialysis, but many people suffering from diabetes and other serious health problems would benefit. After receiving encouragement from the director of nursing, I decided to apply.

Desiring transparency, I took a risk by informing my boss of my intentions to leave the business office. With a spirit of acceptance she told me she'd never stand in my way. She said she'd sensed my desire for change and growth and understood it. She told me she appreciated my honesty and that she'd miss me. Touched, I explained that I believed I'd developed some leadership skills over the past few years that could be put to good use; that my decision wasn't personal.

While my boss completed a transfer form required by the human resources department, I updated my resume. I didn't know how to present my transferable skills in a way that attracted the reader. I didn't know how to convince decision-makers that I could do the new job. In short, I had no idea how to market *me*. But I did the best I could and submitted the skeletal document along with a cover letter and two of my published articles. Then I waited.

At the end of October I received written notification that I'd been selected as a candidate for the first round of interviews. Because I had little experience in interview settings, I was nervous. Fortunately the director of nursing, soft-spoken and gentle, helped me relax. She reviewed the diverse job duties and asked a series of pointed questions. She expressed interest in the articles. I talked about how my teaching experience and organizational abilities would benefit staff, colleagues, and workflow. After forty-five minutes she stood up, shook my hand, and promised to contact me once the clinical director for the renal unit came on board. I left her office on a positive note.

Just before Thanksgiving I was called for an interview with the new clinical director. Immediately I liked her. She was about my age, energetic, and kind. She asked me many of the same questions I'd been asked during the first interview. I, too, asked questions and pursued certain topics in greater depth. At the end she assured me that she and the director of nursing would make a final selection within a week or two. As I returned to work in the outpatient billing office, I realized that I just wanted the process to come to a close. From the time the ad had appeared in the paper it had been going on for nearly six months. Wrapping up had become more important than winning.

Though subtle, a bit of fear had crept into the picture by that point. I had started to doubt my ability to function effectively as a manager. After all, I'd never supervised employees in my career. I'd never been responsible for productivity and results beyond my own. In this interim period I felt some inadequacy. Briefly I considered withdrawing my name from the candidate pool. But I wasn't a quitter, so I hung in.

A few days after the holiday weekend I got a call from the secretary for the business office department head. She asked me to report for yet another conversation the next morning. This request caught me off guard, as I'd been under the impression that the interview process was complete. For me, there was more at stake in this particular interaction than in the previous ones. First and foremost, in her role at the hospital the department head ultimately determined whether I continued to be on the payroll in her department or not. Second, whatever she communicated to the other decision-makers would carry significant weight. Her perceptions and feelings about me mattered.

When I arrived at her door she asked me to sit down. Then she informed me that she'd decided to put away her usual ten questions and simply talk to me on a casual level. She told me that she couldn't talk to everybody the way she was going to talk to me. I didn't know what that meant, but I let her take the lead. For the first time in seven years we had the opportunity to learn a lot about each other personally and professionally. I'd always felt intimidated by this physically large, loud, and demanding leader. After more than an hour she folded her hands, leaned across her desk, and said in a measured, low voice, "You've been a team player from the beginning. You gave more than you had to give on many occasions. I'd be pleased to work with you if you get the position." Hearing those words was the best part of the meeting.

In early December I attended an open house at the dialysis center. The hospital CEO, one of the vice presidents, and the newly appointed clinical director welcomed all visitors into the building. A festive mood permeated the warm environment. This was a big day, and the media was present to help celebrate. After I toured the facility lovely refreshments were served. Part of me felt a little uncomfortable, not yet knowing if I had a job there. I tried to blend into the crowd.

A week later I reached into my mailbox at home and pulled out an envelope with the hospital's return address on it. My heart sank. I assumed I was holding a rejection letter. For several days I hadn't been able to shake the feeling that I'd not been chosen. Now it was true. Upon tearing open the envelope I saw that my intuitive sense had become a fact. Naturally I wondered who had gotten the job.

My heart pounded. For eight long months I had anticipated and pondered a job change that wasn't going to happen. Again I felt stuck. When I told a friend about the outcome, she said they didn't know what they had passed up. I appreciated her generosity. Someone else in my life at the time advised me to accept it as a sign that I was to go in a different direction. Somewhat discouraged, I poured myself into baking Christmas cookies and writing cards. I needed to take my mind off what seemed like a failure.

Just after the new year a colleague informed me that none of the office manager candidates had been chosen to fill the position. Decision-makers were back to square one. Puzzled, I asked why. She told me that none of us had fit the bill, however they defined it. Another ad would be placed in the newspaper and the search process would continue. Official opening of the center was to be delayed. Instantly I wondered what I'd lacked. Finally, days later, I laid the whole thing to rest by concluding that senior management obviously preferred someone with a great deal more experience than I had then. That was okay.

In the meantime I focused on facilitating the bereavement support group I and several others had organized and launched at my church back in the fall of 1987, six months after Don's death. The idea had originated during a conversation between a prominent member and the deacon. When I learned of this proposed project, I expressed a strong desire to help bring it to fruition. I viewed it as a perfect way to utilize my loss and grief experiences to benefit other people.

Once the pastor was pulled into the dialogue, a small committee was formed to discuss the group's purpose and plan logistics. Three of the four of us had suffered at least one significant loss. But the woman who dominated the initial meeting conversation was death naïve. Her words, though spoken intelligently and eloquently, sounded hollow. It occurred to me that perhaps she thought she understood grief without having lived it. I sat there in my chair, turned off by her opinions but committed to remaining tolerant for the sake of the project. At my suggestion the committee agreed to hold the first monthly support group meeting before Christmas because most grieving people find that time of the year to be especially challenging. We also decided to expand our reach by including parishioners from the nine sister churches in our local deanery.

A dozen men and women participated in the first gathering. I had accepted the assignment of providing a few introductory remarks in which I explained why we believed such a group had value. Over coffee and cookies in the conference room I invited folks to tell us their names and share their personal experiences in whatever way felt comfortable to them. I modeled what we wanted them to do by sharing my own story first. As people talked, I tried to maintain a tone of sensitivity and warmth. Some people finished their stories without showing any emotion; others broke down somewhere in the middle. We discussed the upcoming holidays and how we might approach them in light of our circumstances.

Afterwards one man took me aside and said that he sensed great strength radiating from me. A woman living with a very ill husband who refused to see doctors thanked me for allowing her to sit in silence and for accepting her without asking questions. I tucked a little piece of paper with my name and phone number on it into her hand. I wanted her to know she could call me between meetings. As time went on, I encouraged others to phone me, and I reached out to them. It wasn't unusual for me to spend forty-five minutes to an hour offering person-alized support to a hurting member of the group.

One of my older friends, recently widowed, attended the second meeting despite being somewhat resistant to the idea. At the end she confided that perhaps group sharing could help her make the adjust-ments she couldn't escape. I agreed. I'd received feedback that already a few people had found the meetings to be both comforting and useful. I'd been thinking about offering short presentations on various topics at some of the meetings. These would provide a focus for meaning-ful discussion.

Four months into the bereavement support group meetings I observed a drop in attendance. One woman openly criticized my lead-ership style. When I asked her if she'd like to serve as co-facilitator, she quickly declined. I didn't know what else to do with the hostile situation that was clearly brewing. Soon another woman complained to me about the group. When I urged her to describe the specific reasons for her anger, she walked out. My initial reaction centered on doing whatever was required to keep the peace. But I didn't believe that was possible. Frustrated and baffled, I remembered a number of troubles Don had encountered with INSIGHT when he led it. Often those problems bothered him enough to disturb his sleep. My empathy for him—and for anyone doing this kind of work—suddenly increased.

I made an appointment to speak with the pastor. He wasn't surprised I'd called. After listening carefully to my tales of woe, he wasted no time telling me that a power struggle existed between me and one of the women. He told me that although I hadn't created it, I had to deal with it. He went on to say that because the other woman was running from her grief, she was annoyed with the seriousness of the meetings. He educated me about general adult group dynamics and about how most groups, regardless of purpose, wax and wane. At the conclusion of our conversation he recommended that the planning committee reconvene and discuss these issues. If resolution didn't occur, he warned, the bereavement group might dissolve.

On a warm weekday afternoon in the midst of my private discouragement I serendipitously ran into one of the men in the support group and he complimented me on the excellent job I was doing. His comment reaffirmed my efforts and commitment. I considered altering direction, adding some variety to the experience. Perhaps social outings interspersed with regular meetings could make a positive difference.

In the spring I arranged a dinner at a local restaurant and a picnic at a park. Over hot dogs and baked beans I interrupted light conversation to share some thoughts and observations. Then I invited participant comments. A few women admitted that over time the meetings dragged them down and triggered tears they preferred not to shed. I proposed that individuals needed to determine for themselves when to leave the group. In general people said they were glad the group existed and that it had provided an opportunity to develop new friendships with folks who understood their pain. They suggested that the clergy should proactively make referrals, inviting newly grieving parishioners to join. After twenty minutes of discussion I told them with some emotion that no one had learned more from the group than I had. It was a humbling experience.

In late summer I scheduled another appointment with the pastor to tell him that I thought the original group had run its course. It had met for approximately seven months, and I felt the members had outgrown it. I told him that although measuring success with something as subjective as that was difficult, I believed the bereavement support group had value. When I finished speaking, he advised me to start another group with new people and run it for four months. He proceeded to talk about the benefits of an established end point. Assuring me of assistance from the church secretary, he also gave me permission to contact all survivors of deceased parishioners from the previous year to encourage their participation.

A few weeks later I launched the second group. Seven people attended the first meeting. It was interesting that four were familiar faces who had elected to return despite their mixed feelings about the meetings. But three were new faces floundering in the depths of fresh grief. Afterwards one woman tugged at my sleeve in the alley as I walked toward my car. She wanted a hug. Sobbing, she told me she wasn't like the rest of the people in the group. Her situation was different. I nodded with a subtle, knowing smile. I'd learned firsthand and from others that everybody thinks their loss situation and feelings are unique. But I'd also learned that isn't entirely true. Common denominators exist. I urged her to keep coming back and allow the group sharing to help her heal.

To my delight she and quite a few others showed up for the next meeting. But the seats were empty again the following month. I wasn't sure what had happened. When I followed up with several people by phone, I discovered that even they couldn't explain their absence. As I reflected on the circumstances, I realized that I'd grown bored with having to pull teeth to motivate folks to take advantage of a free opportunity that could serve them. It wasn't long before I decided to pull the plug.

In January of 1986 I dreamed a strange dream. Someone had asked me to climb a very high ladder in a hotel. Afraid of heights in an open setting, I momentarily considered declining the request. For some unknown reason, though, I accepted the challenge and proceeded to climb. My nerves jittered. Yet the higher I climbed, the more I sensed a quiet assurance that I'd succeed without falling. I felt protected. When I reached the top of the ladder, I looked down at the floor and all around. Without a doubt I'd accomplished something I never would have imagined possible—something I wouldn't have thought about doing in the first place. It amazed me.

Three months later I shocked myself by answering an ad for a job I didn't even know existed until I'd read about it in the newspaper. A local community-based nonprofit health organization sought an HIV/AIDS educator, a newly created position at the agency intended to benefit the county. Three years previously Don and I had tuned in to a radio show about AIDS featuring a local physician who supposedly was an expert on the disease. That particular doctor believed HIV was a potentially serious health problem capable of radically altering societal behavior, though most people outside of the country's major east- and west-coast cities had never heard of it. I took a very big leap and sent my resume to the executive director of the organization.

I'd read in a book once that all of us need to experience and endure certain losses to move us into the next phase of our lives. It was indisputable that my life had changed because Don had died, but it had not ended. I had traveled a difficult road, and the requirements of that road transformed me. I was indeed different. And because I was different, I was ready for a different future not yet defined. I now knew more clearly who I was and who I was not, so it was time to flesh out this new identity.

PART II

Positioned to Lead

Chapter 11
TAKE RISKS

My life changed dramatically in June of 1989. It felt like someone had drawn a line in the sand and I'd just stepped over that line into a brand new world. After two lengthy, meticulous interviews, the executive director of the community-based health organization offered me the job of HIV/AIDS educator/coordinator. She believed without a doubt that I was the right person to create a community-based AIDS program. Intuitively I knew that my entire life—especially the previous decade—had been a rigorous training ground for this calling. Although I knew little about AIDS, in the depths of my stomach I felt ready to plunge into some very dark, rough waters.

My enthusiasm for this unique professional opportunity ran high. But there was risk involved. If I hadn't married a person with juvenile diabetes and gone through what I had because of it, perhaps I would have declined the offer. I had learned to take various risks while living with and caring for Don, but this was different because the program funding through the Pennsylvania Department of Health could be temporary. The position might terminate after a couple of years. Nothing was certain. During my second interview I candidly laid this issue on the table. I had no prior experience with paychecks that were distributed late—or not at all. As a single woman with few financial assets, I worried about a sudden crash. The executive director listened carefully as I revealed my fears. Afterwards she looked deeply into my eyes and said, "It is time for you to spread your wings. Sometimes we must take a chance and trust."

With butterflies in my stomach I resigned from my job at the hospital in early July. In the exit interview with the human resources representative I took another risk by talking openly about what I viewed to be the major ongoing problems in my office. Although my remarks were heard, I recognized that I might burn bridges. If that was the case, I realized I was fine with it. I knew in the depths of my being that I'd never go back. At the end of the conversation the man told me he valued my articulate observations and insights and wouldn't hesitate to rehire me. I never found out if anything changed because of what I'd said.

From the beginning I had a hunch I'd be immersed in all kinds of risk through my work at the agency. While risk-taking in general still unnerved me, it no longer paralyzed me. Before landing the job I couldn't have defined those specific risks, but it didn't take long to identify them. In addition to the reality of soft funding, I took a risk just by assuming a job title with the word *AIDS* in it. In addition to educating the community about the disease, collecting and developing literature, and establishing a referral network among county-wide human service organizations, I was required to provide case management and support for persons with HIV and their families. Some of these duties put me in direct contact with infected individuals. I soon learned there were people who disliked being around me because of that element of my job. As a result I endured a certain amount of social discrimination over the course of the next five years.

During a telephone call one day my brother expressed concern for my physical safety. Far removed from the field of HIV/AIDS, he had limited knowledge about transmission modes and factors. Because he and many others didn't understand how difficult it actually would be for me to contract the virus by doing non-medical work, scores of folks communicated their reluctance to touch me. One woman refused to shake my hand when she met me in a public setting until she had wrapped hers in a cloth handkerchief. An acquaintance admitted hesitation to sit beside me in a restaurant. While dropping off supplies at a local bar, the owner requested that I set the bag on the counter instead of handing it to him. Twelve months into this journey I concluded things were bad when the city mayor, in a closed venue, asked if I was aware that simply brushing against my clothing disturbed certain people she didn't name.

Although it never happened, I wondered if I'd lose some personal friends. I worried that folks would assume I was infected with HIV. After all, I shook hands with my clients and hugged them. Periodically I transported clients in my car. While being ostracized didn't scare me, I wouldn't have enjoyed it. Until I took that job I had never been concerned about my reputation. Yet I wasn't naïve enough to think that working in an AIDS program couldn't cause irreparable damage. In fact, the deeper I immersed myself into the work, the more I became aware of this. Over the years a handful of clients who were willing to reveal their HIV status posed with me for newspaper photographs. I put myself out in the community in a way that most people wouldn't have dreamed of doing.

Political risk became my companion, too. Just educating the public about a disease viewed as the modern plague upset a number of accepted social norms. Distributing condoms and talking about the need to shoot drugs with clean needles raised more than a few eyebrows. In addition, folks questioned my motives for my involvement with drug users and gay men. Did I see illicit drug abuse as a crime or a disease? Did I condone or oppose homosexuality? This sort of probing followed me everywhere. Even among the gay community, skepticism thrived. Why did I choose to work with populations I knew little about? What was in it for me?

The local paper featured a public comment section called "Sound Off." My name appeared often in that column. Occasionally a contributor expressed empathy and praise, but usually these brief communiques spewed venom. A select group of very vocal people repeatedly told the world I'd rot in hell for serving sinful, at-risk clientele. It was ugly. During a private conversation someone close to me pointed out the dangers of my job. He'd obviously thought about them. Though he didn't advise me to quit, he made it clear he felt the heat of the fire. Together we speculated about how long I'd willingly burn.

Ire came from licensed professionals, too. When I addressed county physicians, dentists, and morticians about the need to practice universal precautions with all of their patients, demonstrate compassion, and accept HIV/AIDS as an epidemic that might be here to stay, resentment frequently flared. Talking to clergy from diverse religious denominations wasn't any easier. Nobody wanted infected persons in their houses of worship. The truth was that I and my bold messages offended many people. Early in the game I discovered that allowing myself to get emotionally close to dying clients was the least of the risks I faced.

Taking risks is part of leadership. The sooner you learn to become more comfortable with risk, the better you manage it and accept it as a given in your world. Women often shy away from risk-taking because we are raised to avoid it. From the time we are small we are told that we should leave risk-taking to men. We form assumptions that risk is dangerous and unwise.

Yet risk—planned and unplanned—is essential to achieving both individual and organizational success. There is no getting around it. Taking reasonable risks has a price, though. It requires stepping outside of your comfort zone to get something better or do something bigger. It requires thinking about all that could go wrong and deciding if what you want is worth the stress and the possibility of failure. Risk-taking asks you to trust the process of life and the old saying that most things have a way of working out. It is about stretching. As a leader, you must let yourself stretch.

At the time of this writing I've identified seven benefits to risk-taking. I want to share them with you now:

1. It invites you to see opportunity.

Reframe the risk with which you grapple as a chance to advance yourself and/or your organization. For example, terminating a stagnant or problem staffer can create space for someone ideal. Delegating more responsibility to a trusted team member can free you up to focus on your priorities. Trashing a familiar, cumbersome process that slows workflow can pave the way for developing something that's truly efficient.

2. It boosts your self-confidence.

The more often you take risks and succeed, the more confident you feel. Once on the other side, you realize you survived. Further, sometimes you discern without a shadow of a doubt that you must do what is necessary for the health and well-being of your organization. Initiating difficult, critical conversations with employees, volunteers, or board members isn't easy; you risk altering the relationship or prompting the person to quit. But you take the risk because you know it's right.

3. It helps you learn and grow.

When you take risks, you don't stay stagnant. Often you expand your skill set. Saying yes to something you've never tried before takes you into a new domain. Sign up for an advanced computer class in which everybody is ten or twenty years younger than you. Agree to write a public service announcement for your agency's latest offering. Accept the challenge of preparing and delivering a twenty-minute speech for your company's annual meeting.

4. It allows you to shine as a leader.

Very few people like to take risks. Consider the folks in your professional circle. How do they really feel about risk-taking? You can set yourself apart from others by making a conscious decision to say or do something they wouldn't. For example, many people aren't willing to take a stand for an idea or action when the stakes are high. Develop a habit of doing this with issues that count. True leaders don't hide.

5. It opens up possibilities.

Today most professionals spend countless hours in meetings during a typical workweek. What exactly are you contributing while you sit there? Stop accepting everything you hear at face value. Take a risk and ask essential questions that probe the layers of complex problems and dilemmas. Dare to make bold observations about team function, product development, or work culture. Inspiring people to think more deeply empowers them to identify and connect with a host of possibilities they might never have considered.

6. It encourages you to become more proactive.

Taking small risks that have minor consequences attached to them is one of the best ways you can move from a predominantly reactive mode into a more deliberate, proactive approach to your job responsibilities. Tired of all the petty interruptions each day? Close your office door for one hour. Train your staff to honor this signal that you are absorbed in tasks and projects that require your undivided attention. Such a strategy helps you reclaim some focused time without damaging key relationships.

7. It supports your efforts to overcome the fear of failure.

Every time you take a risk and succeed, your fear of failure loses power. You learn to disregard the stigma often associated with defeat, collapse, deficiencies, missteps, and botch. Willingly you shed childhood assumptions like "only losers fail," "one failure leads to another," and "all failure is bad." You realize that occasionally smart, educated people do fail; that trying new ideas can be good; and that the negative impact of most failures is only temporary. You learn to put failure into a healthy perspective.

> To what extent do you take risks in your leadership role? How regularly do you take them? Where and how would you like to take more risks? Which of the benefits above have you personally observed and experienced in your career thus far?
>
> By the way, don't forget to grab my free assessment entitled "How Is Your Loss Keeping You Stuck?" To download it go to www.launchinglives.biz/pdfs/Bookassessment.pdf.

Between 1996 and 2008 I served as the executive director of a four-teen-county HIV/AIDS planning coalition in Pennsylvania, an ideal position for me after all of my hand-dirtying, community-based AIDS program experience. Ten years into this job that involved regular, close interaction with Pennsylvania's Department of Health and numerous statewide colleagues, Donna, one of my peers from another coalition, called me out of the blue while I was sitting at my desk eating lunch. She had gotten to know me well as a result of observing my meeting facilitation and problem-solving skills in action. I had also provided spot-on professional direction and guidance to her privately on many occasions. During this telephone conversation she shocked me by suggesting that I strongly consider opening a coaching business for persons in management and leadership roles. She said she'd been mulling it over for a while and had reached the conclusion that much as I'd be missed by everybody in the HIV/AIDS world, the time had come for me to use my natural talents and expertise in a new way. As I listened to her, I nearly choked on my sandwich.

I did not come from a family of entrepreneurs. In fact I didn't know any entrepreneurs personally. Politely I told Donna I'd think about it. But to be honest, I felt overwhelmed. Despite those feelings, I couldn't ignore the seed that had been planted. Immediately after the new year in 2008, approximately eighteen months after that career-altering telephone call, I registered for an executive coaching course. Four weeks into the program I fell in love. The rest was history.

In June of that year I started Launching Lives—a career development specialty company targeting executives and managers. Having no prior formal business training or experience, I took a huge risk. When the U.S. economy tanked in the fall, I fully grasped the extent of that risk. For a couple of years I lived in chronic fear of loss and failure, barely putting one foot in front of the other. Looking back, maybe that wasn't such a bad thing. It allowed me to empathize with many of my clients on a personal level.

One of my first clients, Lori, contacted me when she finally decided that she needed to leave her demanding, long-term senior management job. Divorced and struggling with cancer, she described herself as insecure with low self-esteem. Tearfully she told me she wasn't sleeping well and her energy level had reached an all-time low. Her ability to concentrate was compromised. For months she hadn't been doing her best work. Life's curve balls had poked holes in her confidence, and she admitted to being grievously afraid of new situations. Realizing her sanity depended on it, Lori expressed interest in hiring me to release her paralysis and get unstuck. She yearned for professional employment with less stress and more freedom, but she doubted that she could manifest this desire on her own.

From the beginning of the coaching engagement I noticed that Lori was operating from a deep vulnerability and almost palpable weakness. Although she had adjusted well after her divorce, she exhibited signs that the cancer—supposedly in remission—was wearing her down. A friend assured her that she was worthy of exploring professional opportunities that would allow her to demonstrate her exemplary leadership skills, but Lori questioned if she really possessed the skill set with which her friend credited her. She wondered if the woman was simply being kind.

At the time we started working together, Lori had hit rock bottom. She felt it, and I knew it. Exasperated, she lamented what she perceived to be a failure on her part to climb the ladder in her career. Although her job responsibilities over the last decade had expanded her competencies, she saw no way to advance within the organization. She believed she was trapped.

Further, Lori viewed herself as incompatible with her supervisor, whom she portrayed as severely controlling, verbally abusive, and mentally unstable. She told me her boss was intelligent, knowledgeable, and indisputably committed to the mission and strategic plan, but she was paying too high a price by continuing to work for her. Her boss's random tirades—generally precipitated by minor incidences—negatively affected not only Lori's morale, but also her ability to think. She confided that she needed a supervisor with a different personality and very different traits.

For six months I coached Lori intensely. My charge was to move her forward, and I was committed to it. Initially I recommended that she stop fighting her boss, her cancer, her disappointments, her feelings of being overwhelmed. These relentless fights were compounding her misery. I taught her to view all of these things through a neutral lens. I reminded her that she had choices; that she could choose to make peace with her disease, choose to leave her job, and choose to find a more fulfilling work environment. Lori hadn't thought of her situation in that way. A large part of her viewed it as fixed, impossible to change. She finally saw that her perception—not the circumstances themselves—caused the biggest problem.

Via assignments and sessions Lori connected to her core intrinsic values, natural strengths, and non-negotiable needs. This was a period of extensive self-discovery. We pinpointed her stress triggers, discussed job preferences, and identified potential professional opportunities for which she would be ideal. As a result of these exercises and conversations Lori began to loosen up. She started to play and dream and hope. She slept through the night. She went out with friends. She laughed. Having noted the shift, I predicted that Lori was on the brink of a breakthrough.

Several months into the work I pushed harder (another type of risk). I explained that the foundation of credible leadership is solid self-leadership. In Lori's case this meant that she had to take charge of her career instead of waiting for inspiration to strike or an opportunity to fall out of the sky. She needed to listen to her heart's desire and own her goal. I invited her to draw a line in the sand and set a drop-dead date for exiting her current position. She tensed upon hearing this. After some deliberation she decided to leave her job three months later—no matter what.

We talked about everything involved with the move. To symbolize the change, I suggested she take home one little personal item from her office each week. This action, Lori said, helped make the upcoming leave-taking more real. Further, it inspired her to assume more responsibility for what she claimed she wanted. And it relieved some stress.

Together we revised Lori's resume, capitalizing on her obvious abundant strengths. Because she hadn't touched the document in a decade, she felt unclear about how to meet present-day state-of-the-art standards. She also admitted that she didn't know how to write an attention-grabbing cover letter that wouldn't end up in the trash can. I provided the necessary instruction, guidance, and support throughout the writing process. Once several versions were completed, I prepared her for job interviews. Finally we role-played the resignation conversation she intended to initiate with her boss.

Lori left her employment on the date she'd set in stone. Although she didn't have another job lined up at the time, she accepted a new professional challenge exactly one month later. In an email to me she communicated her joy, stating that all of her efforts had paid off. Jumping ship had been worth the risk.

Chapter 12

GROW YOUR KNOWLEDGE
AND SKILLS

As soon as I'd accepted the position of HIV/AIDS educator/coordinator, I realized I had a lot to learn. Prior to this job I'd taught remedial reading, sold cars and women's clothes, and applied Medicare payments to hospital patient accounts. I didn't understand much about HIV infection and AIDS disease, I had never provided case management services to clients, and I lacked significant firsthand experience with diverse populations. For the most part my life had been rather sheltered. Suddenly that was going to change.

On several occasions during the two weeks of downtime before I officially started the new job, I camped out at Hershey Medical Center's College of Medicine Library reading as much literature about HIV/AIDS as I could find there. For the short term I felt a strong commitment to increase my knowledge about the subject; for the long term my goal was to become an expert. Once on board at the agency I began to buy a wide variety of books and videos with funding donated by the local Visiting Nurses Association.

As an avid reader and ardent student, immersing myself in shelves of educational materials over the first few weeks didn't seem like work. Zealously I filled my brain with information related to viral transmission methods, physical symptoms, and HIV testing. I studied the disease progression process, opportunistic infections associated with

HIV/AIDS, and the limited available drug therapies. It wasn't long until the community identified me as someone who knew more about HIV/AIDS than anyone else in the county—including most general medical practitioners. In fact, within months of the program's commencement a couple of family doctors and a resident physician called me at the office to ask my advice about when to prescribe the only FDA-approved antiretroviral medication for their patients who were HIV-positive. I interpreted that as a sign of professional respect.

People had also expressed high regard for my knowledge of juvenile diabetes while Don was alive. From my youth I had been the type of person who insisted on knowing the whole truth about things; complex, troubling topics were no exception. I didn't shy away from them. This trait set me apart from many people. As Don's health deteriorated, I proactively sought explanations for unexpected events as well as answers to our ongoing routine questions.

Throughout Don's dying phase I used my book learning to expand my caregiving skills. For example, I needed to learn how to deal with him in the aftermath of mini-strokes, during insulin shocks, and in periods of neuropathy pain. I needed to become proficient in post-surgical at-home healing procedures for his eyes and toe. While I didn't like some of these tasks, I had to do them to ensure desired outcomes.

On the day I met my first client who was infected with HIV, four weeks into the new job, I accepted responsibility for learning how to case-manage effectively. Personal visits to a well-established neighboring county's community-based AIDS program taught me the basics related to conducting intakes, making appropriate service referrals, and determining relevant continuing support. Moreover, there were special reporting forms to complete for the regional HIV/AIDS planning body organized by the Department of Health; I had to learn how to supply the requested data correctly because inaccurate numbers skewed statewide statistics.

Although I'd led a support group at my church, that activity was not part of an employer's formal job description. Quickly I saw that I needed to develop formal facilitation skills. I took steps to do that by watching videos, attending trainings, and talking to seasoned sister staff members in other locations. I also interviewed potential recipients

of those services to gain input from them about their criteria for meaningful meetings. As the HIV/AIDS program grew, I actually launched
multiple support groups: one for individuals who were infected, one
for family members, and one for those grieving for clients who had
died. Eventually I established a group exclusively for women who were
infected and one for prison inmates who were HIV-positive. These
groups evolved based on need.

The client groups, typically held bimonthly, challenged me most.
Attendance waxed and waned. Sometimes illness or fatigue kept people
away. Occasionally folks stayed home because of their frustration with
other members in the group. Further, I found it difficult to satisfy everyone's interests pertaining to meeting focus. Topics that some clients
wanted to discuss didn't appeal to others. In retrospect, attendee expectations were often unrealistic—every meeting could not deliver what
every client wanted.

For me, the various support group settings emphasized the need to
grow my understanding of Hispanic culture, the intravenous-drug-user
mindset, and life in prison. By taking this job I'd entered an unfamiliar world. Rarely did that world frighten me; rather, on most days it
intrigued me. A year into the work a trusted volunteer admitted over a
meal that originally he'd been both astonished and concerned by what
he perceived to be my conspicuous naïveté about the populations with
whom I'd interact. Annoyed by the chilly boldness of his comment, I
privately vowed to change this.

Of course that type of change didn't happen overnight. It came about
gradually by talking directly with clients and participating in regular
regional AIDS service organization meetings. When I visited people
who were infected, I asked them to educate me about their ethnic mores,
family traditions, and cultural beliefs. They seemed to respect my curiosity and desire to learn. At the substance abuse treatment center where
I provided monthly HIV/AIDS educational sessions geared to individuals in recovery, I listened to scores of personal stories and accountings
of illicit drug use experiences. Over the course of many months my
insight deepened. Once approved to meet with clients in the county jail,
I spent countless hours behind the walls. There administration, staff,
and inmates openly informed me about the protocols, regulations, and

unwritten rules. Frequently I observed the struggles myself. Believe me, over five years I shed whatever innocence I might have had going in.

No leader is perfectly developed. Regardless of our age, credentials, or career phase we always have some knowledge or skill gap. Identifying that gap is essential for our own sakes as well as for the well-being of our businesses and organization. Sometimes we know intuitively where we fall short, feel inadequate, or miss the mark. Other times we become aware of these gaps through constructive or brash feedback from bosses, colleagues, and clients. A problem lies not in having a gap but in choosing to ignore it.

In what areas must you improve because your current employment performance depends on it? In which must you advance because your organization requires it of its leaders? In which is it advisable for you to grow because of your desired short- or long-term career trajectory? In which do you want to grow simply because you are interested? Get clear about your gaps as well as why you are going to address them. Take a look at the following areas:

Hiring and firing
Supervision
Staff development
Delegation
Mentoring
Communication
Time management
Vision
Understanding complex issues
Strategic thinking
Strategic planning
Decision-making
Problem-solving
Crisis management
Personal accountability
Difficult, necessary conversations
Stress management
Listening

Professional image
Responsibility
Public speaking
Self-motivation
Conflict resolution

Professional development requires time, effort, and money. It starts with a decision and continues with commitment. In this new millennium growth is not an option. Take charge of your knowledge bank and skill set and keep them current. Sometimes that means investing your own financial assets or altering your daily routine. Growth can be an inconvenience. But complacency doesn't serve. Produce steadily to retain your leadership position. You must produce, and produce even more at a higher level to move on.

Set your goals and establish criteria for success. Pick a date to dig in your heels. Hire a coach. Refuse to stay stuck. Reject mediocrity. Resist the temptation to coast.

Why bother to increase your knowledge and grow your skills? Here are seven big benefits:

1. It enhances job performance.

If you aren't conducting regular annual employee evaluations, you are avoiding an important part of your job. Staff members deserve formal feedback, and organizations owe it to themselves to track individual strengths and weaknesses. Lack of know-how, outdated process, personal awkwardness, and time constraints are poor excuses for putting this duty on the back burner. Upgrade your own performance by dealing directly with whatever blocks you from fulfilling this managerial obligation. Then schedule the reviews.

2. It conveys commitment to growth.

Are you reluctant to delegate tasks and projects to others who can do them well? Although this can be a lifelong habit, it's more likely a form of control that you should release. Start small. For example, you could select someone to represent you at an inconsequential meeting. Solicit agenda highlights later. Decide to delegate at least one item on your to-do list each week. Tell people what you are doing and why. Let your staff, boss, and board see that you are committed to growth.

3. It influences others.

It's a fact: The better you communicate, the greater your influence. Communication is a sizable bucket that contains words, volume, tone, speed, pitch, listening skills, facial expressions, body stance, and gestures. In a typical week you probably utilize a variety of communication modes such as emails, phone calls, text messages, memos, letters, and face-to-face contacts. People form an impression of you based largely on how you communicate with them. If you're not getting optimal results from folks in your work environment, you might need to learn some new and different communication skills.

4. It positions you as an expert.

A basic understanding of any subject or process can move things along in an organization to a certain extent. Today, however, knowledge of the fundamentals may not be enough for real progress to take place. Perhaps you can interpret and implement an already established strategic plan, but you have no idea how to lead key players through the steps to create one. If that's true, you've identified an activity sphere in which it would be wise to advance. Seek formal training and mentoring to reach expert status, and enjoy the fruits of earning your board's trust in this area.

5. It models desired actions and behavior.

Whenever you learn something new and use it to benefit your organization, you send a powerful message. Every time you acquire or expand a skill, you set a positive example for others watching you. Demonstrations of your personal and professional growth give staff and volunteers permission to grow. Having the courage and ability to initiate difficult but necessary conversations as the need arises lets other people know that it's okay for them to do the same.

6. It opens opportunity doors.

Knowledge stagnation and skill stagnation kill careers. If you are serious about landing a promotion, increase your value at work. The person to whom you report has to see consistent evidence of more, bigger, and better contributions from you. One of the most effective ways to prove your readiness to move up is to identify problems, pose several viable solutions, and help resolve those issues. Problem-solving ability is extremely attractive today. Employers look for this skill in the folks they place at the top.

7. It boosts your credibility.

As a leader you appear more credible to the people around you when you make an earnest, focused effort to develop your skill set. Folks take you seriously, tend to believe what you say, and naturally trust you. It's a beautiful thing to experience. For instance, when your staff observes your commitment to hold yourself accountable in situations that matter to them, they discover that respect for their boss comes easily. Consider drawing them into your development process by inviting them to catch you when you drop the ball. Over time, doubts about your motives and ability to deliver are likely to disappear.

How can you minimize or close your knowledge and/or skill gaps? What is your short- and long-term plan? What resources do you need? What is a reasonable first step? By what date do you promise to take that step?

Linda's supervisor, Elizabeth, engaged my services to upgrade Linda's supervisory skills and improve her overall image prior to expanding her management responsibilities. When I asked Elizabeth to describe the areas of challenge in detail, she told me that Linda lacked the confidence to hold those who directly reported to her accountable for their behavior and performance on a consistent basis. She explained that Linda was having trouble as a committee chair, too; people didn't take her seriously enough, often enough. Elizabeth believed that Linda had lots of potential but needed someone to awaken and develop it. I said I'd be glad to help.

As I came to know Linda, I learned that she'd been divorced for several years. By anyone's standards, she functioned well in the world. A licensed health care professional, she'd served in various capacities in a couple of large hospital systems. She worked hard, earned a decent salary, and was valued by many peers. Despite her success, Linda felt inadequate and diminished. She confided that she feared being disliked, getting fired, and navigating new situations. The fact that her husband left her for somebody else had taken a hidden toll.

Chronic stress, office clutter, and often being overwhelmed by responsibilities were additional manifestations of this toll. People who interacted with Linda frequently noticed tension in her neck and jaw. She admitted to rarely taking time out of a busy day for meals. She also told me that she had difficulty falling and staying asleep at night. Shutting off incessant mental chatter about possible failures had become a problem. Responding perfectly to her boss's inquiries about team work progress—telling her precisely what she wanted to hear—was another.

I explained that people build both their confidence and competence muscles through practice. There was only one way to get better at confronting an employee's missed deadlines, and that was to do it every time it happened. I provided Linda with language for initiating and carrying through with those kinds of conversations that also included consequences for continuing unacceptable behavior. After I gave her the tools, I expected her to implement them. During her next coaching session I checked in with her about circumstances that warranted using these scripts as well as her ability to use them effectively.

This work provided a natural segue into learning strategies for functioning more effectively as a committee chair. In this role Linda faced the challenge of motivating participants to follow through with the assignments they had chosen or agreed to accept during meetings. The committee members were not her employees but rather colleagues representing other departments within the larger organization. Holding them accountable required a different approach and style from holding her staff accountable. Boldly I told Linda that she had to elevate her stature in her own mind before others would regard her as a leader worthy of esteem. That statement had a profound effect on her. She never forgot it.

To her dismay, Linda had historically received a fair amount of criticism from members of this committee. She felt they often misinterpreted her input and recommendations. When I asked her to describe her reactions to this criticism, she promptly informed me that when she believed it was not justified she either got defensive or completely shut down. In the heat of the moment she tried to look the person in the eye and maintain a controlled voice tone. She vented frustration over her impulse to speak too fast when nervous. Further, she told me that in some cases when she felt brave, she proactively sought verbal clarification about the other party's viewpoint. Linda admitted that most criticism threw her off balance and she would obsess about it for days. I suggested that she turn down the burner on her tendency to personalize criticism. I also taught her the strategy of interjecting more open-ended, thought-provoking questions into meeting dialogue when she was inclined to make strong statements.

Criticism presented a problem for Linda because her ex-husband had criticized her constantly; she felt scarred by it. During the coaching engagement our examination of criticism evolved into scrutiny about anger and how Linda expressed it in the work environment. We talked about her rigid body posture and the difficulty she had maintaining eye contact and managing voice volume when her ire was raised. Remembering that some folks feared her anger, she lamented her frequent knee-jerk responses to irritating remarks. Such responses, cynical and uncaring, had temporarily alienated various key people over the years. Aware of the destructive impact, Linda openly regretted responding in that way and committed to searching for substitutes that carried less sting.

I cautioned her about damaging her professional image in annoying situations, and gave her tips to adjust her body and her words. I showed her how to move into a contrived neutral zone within her mind until the initial rage passed. Together we identified the negative price paid for allowing anger to dictate her behaviors: loss of respect, punitive repercussions from senior leaders, and career inertia. Linda decided she had to make changes.

After six months I asked her to describe, using specific examples, how life at work had improved as a result of the coaching. With a certain amount of levity in her voice, she told me that she felt—and spoke—like a true leader. She assured me that she was more comfortable in her roles as staff supervisor and committee chair. She felt less like a victim. And best of all? Her boss noticed the difference. When the two of them discussed it privately, Linda beamed. She told me Elizabeth had plans for her. Smiling, I reminded Linda of her primary core value: honesty. I told her that her willingness to get fiercely honest with herself had paved the way for her to grow.

Chapter 13

BUILD PEOPLE, PROGRAMS, PRODUCTS, AND SERVICES

By nature I am a builder. As a child I loved building Lincoln Log houses with my brother. As a teenager I made cakes and pies. Many years later, amid chronic stress, disappointment, boredom, and fear, I built a marriage with Don. So it's not surprising that I devoted my first year in the AIDS Project to building it. Under the umbrella of an established community health agency, a certain amount of infrastructure was already in place. Still, I had to put the meat on the bones. As coordinator, I was responsible for creating a viable, multifaceted program that was expected to become the county's go-to entity for HIV/AIDS information and services. From day one I felt the weight of this charge on my shoulders. It comprised both excitement and burden. That never changed, and I learned to live with it.

There were several moving parts—tangible and intangible. I didn't have the luxury of building one to completion before starting another. As I put together a library, I developed relationships with directors from scores of social service organizations. Early on I recognized the significance of drawing people of influence into my work and my world. During private staff meetings my boss and I discussed this often. She and I knew that the success of the program depended on the solidarity of these relationships. For community acceptance and program growth to occur, it was imperative for the movers and shakers to respect, like, and trust me. It was a priority. One individual could not do such a big job alone. I needed a platform of continuous support.

At the same time I was in the process of forming case management and client support systems, too. As the result of purposeful public outreach, a couple of people infected with HIV approached the program a few weeks after I arrived on the scene. I had to be ready to serve them. Identifying this population's needs and lining up resources to meet those needs monopolized my attention in short order. To ensure a partnership that worked for both parties, I made a lot of phone calls to entities that provided mental health services, crisis intervention, food and clothing, drug and alcohol treatment, and housing. When folks who were HIV-positive showed up in my office, most were getting excellent medical care from Hershey Medical Center ten miles away. It was the holistic approach to care that generally wasn't happening. My clients were seeing an infectious disease specialist, yet didn't have enough to eat. Some had access to medications, but nowhere to live. Coordination of services was critical for these people's well-being and safety.

Approximately nine months into the program a client emotionally voiced his concern for infected individuals who either couldn't afford an apartment or whose families had thrown them out on the street because they perceived them to be a health hazard. He believed that a nomadic lifestyle led to trouble. I agreed. In that moment the idea for a shelter was born. I gave an overview of the situation to the AIDS Task Force, which consisted of more than fifty community professionals representing a wide variety of fields. It didn't take long for members to see evidence of a swelling problem.

By the fall of 1990 the group formed a Housing Task Force within itself, and I was urged to participate. This cluster of eight people, which included an interested lawyer, began to write letters to churches and area businesses requesting financial support for a proposed AIDS shelter. One month later my supervisor accompanied me to a dedication ceremony for a neighboring county's AIDS boarding home and hospice. By attending this event we learned much more about starting and operating this type of facility. Soon the Housing Task Force invited personal-care-boarding-home experts to meetings and scheduled appointments to tour several of these places. Some of my clients recommended the name Wellspring for our potential house. A savings account bearing that name was opened to deposit donations we collected.

In the beginning of the new year things moved quickly. The Housing Task Force wrote a mission statement, goals, objectives, and bylaws for the project. Letters introducing the concept of AIDS-specific housing were prepared for political officials, a logo for all literature was designed, and a brochure was drafted. Incorporation and nonprofit organization status papers were completed, signed, and submitted to state government agencies. Once summer arrived, the group identified possible funding sources for the purchase of a property, construction, renovations of an existing house, and/or maintenance. In the middle of these efforts I filled out a housing affordability strategy survey related to the county's need for such a shelter and returned it to the chamber of commerce. I also contacted a newspaper reporter about doing a feature article on the group's work.

The article, published in July, made the project seem more real to those of us involved with it. But it stirred the pot, too. On a September evening I met with the board of directors of a family shelter that refused to admit one of my female clients. The board president kept insisting that they had an obligation to their other residents. One person stated angrily that he knew all about AIDS and that nothing I said would change his mind about not allowing people who were HIV-positive to stay at their facility. I noticed a number of people tuning me out. At the end of the meeting perspiration was rolling down my back; I knew the board had decided to bar my clients from receiving their services. The board president, exasperated, proposed that each member of the AIDS Task Force should take a person who was infected into his or her home to set an example. His eyes bored into mine. "Tell them what I suggested, then come back here to share your experiences after you've done it," he said. I left frustrated but more determined than ever to build that AIDS house.

A long haul followed. Fundraisers were planned and realized. The Housing Task Force became a board of directors, and appointed officers and created committees. One committee rolled up their sleeves and applied for grants. Another intensely pursued available suitable properties and attended testy zoning hearings and heated neighborhood meetings. As I got out of my car to attend one of those meetings at a potential site, I noticed people sitting on their steps and porches watching me carefully. Eyeing a man holding a long stick in his hand, I felt fear. Mindful of the police car parked across the street, I proceeded to walk slowly toward the building being considered for Wellspring. The Personnel Committee wrote a job description for the shelter's chief executive, advertised the position, interviewed candidates, and eventually hired a doctor to fill that role. In September of 1994 a dream came true: settlement on a house in the city finally took place.

Building, by definition, is both a commitment and a process. You can't build people, programs, or services until you fully understand your big *why*. Invest the time to discern that why. You need a clear purpose and maybe a mission. This clarity provides the focus to get you started and the drive to keep you going when the honeymoon ends. Rewarding as it is, building can be hard. It asks something of you that perhaps you're reluctant to give.

Building requires passion, persistence, and plans. It also requires knowledge and skill. I learned this firsthand as I built the AIDS Project, developed a volunteer program, and helped build Wellspring. Building takes energy and effort, patience and grit. I was surprised when I saw that it called for a willingness to be vulnerable, too, and open to making mistakes, correcting course, and bearing attacks. In most cases building cannot happen without support from colleagues, boards, and community partners. Sometimes it takes money—more than you thought. Building is not for the fainthearted. I know.

There are potential roadblocks to building anything, whether it's emerging leaders, boards of directors, products, programs, services, or something of bricks and mortar. You are wise to identify these obstacles before you commence. If you do, you can save yourself and your organization a lot of frustration, disappointment, and time. Blocks come in the form of individuals, groups, circumstances, and personal limitations, to name a few. As a leader, it's your job to anticipate the resistance of naysayers. It's your duty to proceed with definitive, step-by-step plans. It's your obligation to ensure consistent funding. Stay grounded in realistic expectations for progress and results. Manage politics, morale, and fatigue. The truth is that blocks inherently exist with everything you build; it's what you do with them that counts.

Having built several rather significant things throughout my diverse and lengthy career, I can tell you that there are obvious as well as obscure benefits to the act of building. I want to share these opportunities with you now:

* **Respond to an organizational, community, or global need.**

Responding to an existing need—internal or external—can bring great satisfaction to all parties involved. Through your efforts, human beings receive something of value to them. Have your employees expressed interest in an onsite mentoring program to grow their skills? The entire organization in addition to the individuals involved will profit from building one. Has your community talked about creating an after-school program for elementary-aged children? By building such a program you keep kids off the streets, boost their self-esteem, provide help with homework, and feed them at the same time.

* **Provide something people want.**

Unless you are prepared to lose them, find ways to retain people with high potential in the workplace. These people want to be fully engaged, and they expect you to invest in their professional development. If your company doesn't currently have an employee wellness program and folks are asking why, consider building one. When those on your payroll exercise, eat healthfully, shed pounds, and schedule regular medical checkups, everybody wins. Designing that staff bonus program that many have requested for years might serve as an ideal incentive for actualizing higher sales.

* **Do/Make something better than competitors.**

Whatever you decide to build, you now have the chance to do it better than anybody else. It's an opportunity to excel and shine. You can break a record or make history. Whether it's adding a service to your list of insurance offerings, constructing houses in a brand new neighborhood, or opening a shelter for abused women, you can ensure that YOURS stands apart from that of your competitors.

* **Foster cooperation and collaboration.**

If you think about it, building rarely happens in a vacuum. It usually brings people with diverse ideas and skills together to accomplish something distinct. The act of building allows everybody involved to contribute certain resources. This increases capacity, saves money and time, and reduces waste. By leveraging each party's best, you strengthen your deliverables. Further, a natural checks and balances system exists within collaboration, and there is a broader understanding of the big picture.

* **Experiment.**

This might surprise you: Building a program, product, or service can be viewed as a stimulating, provocative experiment. Building is a highly creative process that invites you to celebrate your boldness and appetite for adventure. It lets you test a theory or assumption, discover what works and doesn't work, or demonstrate expertise and talent. Dare to build and watch yourself and others bloom.

* **Create community.**

Community can mean your team or your town. Building something provides a laser focus that unites people through a common purpose. This unity generates initial and ongoing buy-in, which leads not only to more folks promoting what you build, but also to more folks using it. With a sense of belonging, participants band together to form a stable support system for each other and a guardrail against failure. Creating community is likely the most important key to success.

* **Suit yourself.**

Occasionally you need to build something that meets your specific needs instead of trying to make do with what's comfortable or available. For example, get rid of a product that isn't selling and build one that does. Or clean out the dead wood from your board and bring on people who demonstrate commitment to your mission. Perhaps creating your own employee evaluation process and forms rather than using a boiler-plate system is the best way to go. That way you're sure to cover all that matters related to performance and behavior. Forcing a square peg into a round hole usually doesn't work.

* **Immerse yourself in something bigger than you.**

One of the greatest beauties of building is the privilege to absorb yourself in something beyond the normal scope of work. Reaching for the stars, near or far, is an amazing experience. If you haven't done it in your professional life yet, think of something that beckons you to realize it. Building can be a kind of calling. Sit quietly and listen to your intuition to identify what it is you are to build.

> What do you need or want to build? How can that person, program, product, or service make a real difference? When do you plan to start? What resources are both essential and desired? How can you jump over, go around, or manage potential roadblocks to success?

Over coffee in a local restaurant, Angela became a client of mine immediately after the holiday season ended. She'd scheduled a meeting with me because the previous year had been awful for her business for a number of reasons. Staff morale was low, individual roles and responsibilities were blurred, and a viable strategic plan didn't exist. Things were so bad that she toyed with firing a testy employee. She wanted to trust the people who worked for her but found she couldn't under current circumstances. With frustration and shame she described tread-mill-type weeks that left her totally exhausted. Tasks were getting done and money was being made, but as the owner charged with overseeing all operations, Angela lacked streamlined, high-functioning systems designed to boost quantity and quality of work and minimize stress. Difficult as it was to admit, she said she needed to grow and demon-strate leadership skills that generated tangible and observable results. She needed to build a cooperative, cohesive team capable of deliver-ing outcomes in alignment with her expectations. Something had to change soon.

When I first met Angela I saw an attractive, well-groomed, middle-aged woman dressed in stylish clothes. As we shook hands, her eyes twinkled and she smiled warmly. She struck me as a positive, sincere professional who appreciated herself, had her life in order, and knew where she was going. My initial impression also included imagin-ings of her being born into wealth and enjoying the life of a princess while growing up. As I worked with her, I gradually learned that some of my assumptions were wrong. Beneath her pleasant nature Angela had a loud inner critic, a marked perfectionistic streak, and a strong need to be liked that stemmed from unhealthy family-of-origin issues. Micromanaging task completion and second-guessing many of her own decisions, she wasted time and energy that might have been spent on business development activities or staff mentoring. Often incon-veniencing herself, she took care of those who reported to her directly as if they were family. She was a people-pleaser and feared expressing negative emotions even when appropriate. Supervision, especially the confrontational and disciplinary parts of it, caused her to feel anxious. Because Angela was an intelligent, capable woman, I was determined to help her turn the situation around.

In my opinion Angela's parents' typical interactions with her had marred her ability to trust, which manifested in the workplace, and her sense of self—just enough to erode her confidence in certain areas. Further, their expectations of her seemed unreasonable. I wondered if Angela had had a real childhood, but I never asked. She'd been raised in a household that clearly emphasized performance and skewed the definition of love. It had taken a toll.

At the beginning of the coaching engagement I conducted a simple assessment of Angela. During private phone conversations I interviewed each of her employees, using the same set of questions, to uncover her strengths, unique talents, weaknesses, and essential areas for growth. I concluded that her staff liked and respected their boss, but believed she needed to learn when to take charge and when to let go. Her staff members said they needed a list of defined goals, clarity about what success looked like for their boss, and metrics to measure productivity. Angela and I discussed the results and I suggested she accept them as useful feedback to guide our work together rather than judge them harshly. I noticed that it was difficult for her to do that.

Based on the assessment, I believed that the most important piece to improve was Angela's leadership skills. Everything else, I trusted, would fall into place as she made noticeable progress in this area. I recommended that she meet individually with her employees and ask them what motivated them at work, how they wanted to grow, and what it would take for them to fully support her business goals. We reviewed the answers to those questions during a coaching session. Without hesitation I told Angela that I thought attitude problems and wheel-spinning would come to a halt once the staff understood exactly what they were to do and how it impacted everybody else on the team as well as the bottom line. Moreover, I suggested that all of us sit in the same room and discuss the characteristics of a high-functioning team so that everyone could see where they were on target and where improvements were needed. I explained that the level of team function determined organizational culture.

Two group coaching sessions and a few private phone conversations with each staff person clarified roles, responsibilities, and standards; criteria for individual and team success; and benchmarks for exceeding expectations. As I continued to work with Angela, I emphasized the importance of consistently holding employees accountable for their performance and behaviors. I recommended short, periodic staff meetings in addition to established weekly team meetings. I equipped her with powerful examples of proactive supervisory language.

After several months Angela began to move forward quickly. With my assistance she created essential processes in her business. She developed a basic strategic plan rooted in reality. She increased staff engagement by utilizing their strengths and allowing them to share in the achievement of the goals they set together. Proudly Angela told me that her team was more honest with her and with each other, and that this factor more than any other had enhanced productivity, efficiency, and quality of outcomes. The last time we spoke she was on target for wrapping up a great year.

Chapter 14

FIND YOUR VOICE

When I was a senior in high school I chose a brand new elective course entitled *Public Speaking* even though I was terrified of public speaking. My mother and I had discussed it, and we agreed that the experience could be useful for me even if it made me sweat. Ever since kindergarten I'd been painfully shy. Sadly, by sixth grade my shyness had reached a paralyzing state, and one morning my thirty-something male teacher decided that it was time—and his duty—to move me beyond it. As I entered the classroom I saw a personal message addressed to me scrawled in huge colored chalk letters across the blackboard: "Miss Frey, I expect you to greet me in person when you arrive. Do this every day until further notice." I cringed. By the end of the term I had started to talk. A little bit.

That was a good thing, too, because in high school and college I had instructors who factored class participation into course grades. I felt pressured to answer questions and volunteer opinions about topics de jour. Although I did it, I was uncomfortable. I would have preferred to listen to what everyone else said and keep my thoughts to myself. Had I given in to the temptation, I would have brought home disappointing marks. I wasn't going to accept that. The desire for higher grades motivated me to find my academic voice. My goal to become a teacher inspired me, too.

Years later Don's health decline impelled me to develop other voices hidden deep within. As I practiced those voices in different situations, my confidence grew. With Don I generally used an empathetic voice because he was chronically, then terminally ill. I wanted to be a soothing, comforting presence. However, with medical personnel I sometimes exerted a confrontational voice when I heard ridiculously simplistic plans of action or sensed unacceptable apathy. With a handful of community folks who judged us harshly, on occasion I lapsed into a respectful yet nonetheless defensive voice. I didn't like that voice, but I refused to stand by and allow Don to be victimized by the ignorance of people on the sidelines. And when nothing we experienced made any sense, I used my internal voice of reason to calm myself. I assessed the facts, drew a conclusion, and decided what to do based on history as I recalled it. Frequently my rational voice kept me sane.

All voices have a purpose. They must be employed strategically and judiciously at the right times for the right reasons, especially when you are in a leadership position. Throughout my career I came to understand this truth through various job duties. Certainly I learned it while coordinating the AIDS Project. Just three weeks into the position I presented my first educational session to twenty-five teens. Not having taught formally in eight years, I felt nervous. I'd almost forgotten what it was like to stand in front of a room filled with warm bodies staring at me. Ten minutes later, completely absorbed in my message, the jitters subsided. I'd entered a natural flow, and afterwards everybody clapped. My cheeks flushed. In that moment I knew without a shadow of a doubt that I had a voice—a voice I could use and leverage to make a difference in my world.

Over the course of five years I expanded that repertoire of voices. While delivering hundreds of presentations and speeches to literally thousands of people, I perfected my informational voice. I spoke to social service staff about the epidemiology of HIV infection and how the AIDS Project could benefit their clients. I answered questions for nurses at hospitals and elder care facilities in multiple group settings. Churches invited me to speak from the pulpit. For all seven of the county's school districts I taught age-appropriate classes from grades one to twelve. Some industrial employers requested that I educate their workers. I trained police, probation officers, and emergency management teams concerned about their risk of infection in the line of duty. Community clubs, college students, recovering addicts, youths in juvenile detention, and prison inmates heard me talk about HIV/AIDS. My life, a bit like a fish bowl, was a whirlwind day and night.

With the media I discovered I needed several voices. Reporters, news anchors, and show hosts followed me everywhere. They lusted for the latest scoop on AIDS and supported the project I led. I required an announcer's voice for brief radio interviews, taped and live, that targeted upcoming events and fundraisers, AIDS Task Force meeting content, current statistics, and the progress of the Wellspring housing initiative. Two-hour talk shows that focused on disease treatment information from the annual International AIDS Conference necessitated a combination of factual and conversational voices as listeners called the station to interact with me. Occasionally I participated in these programs with guest specialists who helped field questions from the public about HIV transmission, but mostly I handled them alone. Eventually I wrote and recorded public service announcements about HIV testing, parents educating their children, project hotline services, and new support groups. For these sixty-second, no-nonsense sound bites I had to use a compelling voice. I enjoyed the energy of radio work.

Television, less forgiving because of the visual component, demanded additional skills. I had to look good as well as communicate a clear message with viewer appeal. More than a few times I sat under brilliant, hot studio lights while industry professionals interviewed me on the rise of HIV cases among women, rural nurses' attitudes toward caring for infected persons, and advice for men who'd engaged in sexual relations with a recently arrested prostitute who was HIV-positive. For these sessions I employed the voice of an expert. During a public forum highlighting one of my clients, and another focused on housing, my advocacy voice was most appropriate. I never forgot, though, that TV must entertain—not only through humor but by capturing folks' full attention.

Newspaper feature articles involved a reporter visiting my office. As we discussed details about HIV and nutrition, tree plantings in memory of deceased clients, the purpose of the volunteer buddy program, and the many challenges of dealing with dying people, my influential voice served best. I wanted readers to comprehend the human aspects of this disease, not just the startling numbers associated with it. But my political voice was needed, too. In a job like mine I expected my words to be scrutinized around the clock. I had to be cautious about what I said and how I said it. People watched and judged. Always concerned about causing offense, I walked a tightrope as I told the truth. It took finesse to earn and sustain respect.

In that leadership role—and others going forward—I didn't do it perfectly. Most likely by now you've discovered that you can't and don't employ your voices faultlessly either. But try to use them optimally. Believe me, you can build a leadership platform with your voice. Below is a list of leadership voices along with examples of when to use them and the positive results you might observe.

Authoritative/Directive

This voice, deliberate and sure, is ideal for giving directions or issuing expectations. You sound like the boss. Employees know you mean business and generally deliver. But don't overdo; use it selectively.

Supportive

Calming and gentle, this voice offers assistance when staff members struggle with difficult tasks, work outside their comfort zones, or put in weeks of long hours. While you can use few words, people know you are behind them.

Questioning/Challenging

This voice probes for details about complex issues and seeks clarification when you don't understand somebody's point of view. It can also express disagreement. Never sharp or obnoxious, it is reasonable, receptive, and measured.

Motivating, Inspiring

A motivating voice drives the bus of success. It moves people to step up to the plate and do great things for their companies and careers. Stimulating and uplifting, it lights the fires of possibility. Folks follow your lead because something inside tells them they must.

Rational

Logical and sound, this voice explains reasons behind decisions. It guides employees and board members to look at all sides of a situation. It keeps people rooted in the real world as they conduct business. People might thank you later for helping them avoid costly mistakes.

Confiding

This voice, fueled by trust, selectively shares problems and dilemmas with colleagues and friends. When you unburden yourself, you bestow a great honor upon those with whom you choose to do so. In most cases individuals respond from the depths of their best selves, and you win by gaining valuable insights or solutions.

Appreciative

Generous and grateful, this voice acknowledges team efforts, solutions to problems, kind gestures, and outstanding results. The appreciative voice is spirited and joyful. When you demonstrate genuine appreciation for people's great work and thoughtfulness, you are likely to see evidence of even more of what you acknowledge and praise.

Teaching/Informative

The teaching voice sounds passionate, knowledgeable, and organized. It is ideal for rolling out a new process, explaining a complex concept, or enhancing an essential skill. Sincere and serious, this voice equips staff, board members, and volunteers to do better or different work.

Political

Astute and mindful, this voice should be used when discussing delicate, touchy, or potentially dangerous issues in settings where you can't afford to—or don't want to—offend the parties involved. Learning this particular voice takes time. It is a form of communication art. For most leaders the biggest challenge with the political voice is balancing diplomacy with candor.

Persuasive

A persuasive voice has the power to influence ideas, decisions, behaviors, and actions. It is appropriate for convincing people to believe what you believe, see what you see, and do what you want them to do. It can help them grasp the value of a single project or organizational focus. Sensible, factual, and restrained, this voice can move mountains when applied well.

Disciplinary

Controlled, direct, and respectful, this voice is best used sparingly. When employed too frequently, it loses its punch. Reserve the disciplinary voice for citing poor work performance, broken rules and regulations, and improper behavior. Sharing observations and invoking staff input to make improvements through strategic conversation with this voice can produce positive results.

Announcing

This voice—succinct, pointed, and clear—captures people's attention. It works to introduce a new hire, inform folks of a planned or unplanned change, or disclose an additional company benefit.

Mentoring

Encouraging but candid, the mentoring voice guides unseasoned board members as they acclimate to their role. The voice of experience, it also supports people as they navigate tough situations.

Empathetic

An empathetic voice, externally focused, shows concern for someone else's loss, long hours, or curve ball. Through listening rather than judging, it builds trust.

Confrontational

Assertive but calm and free of hostility, this expressive voice can be used when staffers have done something wrong or are perched to make a mistake. A nonthreatening confrontational voice can be ideal whenever disagreement must occur. A reasonable, respectful approach can help people value a different point of view.

Self-preserving

Employing this voice requires self-esteem and confidence. Neither defensive nor arrogant, it is professionally firm during times of unfair blame, insolence, or character assassination. Generating a memorable personal presence, it lets you be seen and heard as a solid leader when used sparingly and wisely.

> Which voices do you find yourself using most often? Why? Which of your voices tend to get the best results? How do you know this? Which voices must you apply more frequently? Why?

Remember to access my free assessment, "How Is Your Loss Keeping You Stuck?" You can get a copy of it at www.launchinglives.biz/pdfs/Bookassessment.pdf.

I met Lindsey a few years ago standing in the registration line at a leadership recognition event. Although strangers, we struck up a pleasant conversation to pass the time. In closing she looked at me, paused for a moment, and then said she thought she could benefit from coaching. I didn't expect to hear this. A couple of weeks later we got on the phone and discussed her needs. Lindsey told me that as CEO of her small company she had never found her leadership and management voice. This created problems; she hesitated to delegate tasks to staff, avoided necessary confrontations, and shrank from standing up for herself in awkward situations. Lindsey confided that she lacked the confidence to conduct substantial employee evaluations that actually developed people—and held them accountable—in their roles. Repeatedly she found herself accepting too many community volunteer assignments that she didn't want. Being authentic with everybody in her world challenged and scared her, too. When she tried to be real, she tended to express her opinions with intense emotion that alienated those around her. As I listened to her describe these issues, I detected stress in her shallow breathing. Lindsey's inability to stand tall in leadership was like a noose around her neck. She desperately desired to cut that rope.

I assumed that some sort of trauma and loss played a role. When I gently asked her about it, her voice quivered as she divulged examples of excessive parental control, a more recent history of depression, and various forms of abuse in her current long-term marriage. She admitted to being insecure and shut-down. Although Lindsey had sought counseling from a number of recommended psychologists, she informed me that ultimately none of those sessions had altered her deep-seated beliefs about herself or her daily behaviors. I explained that coaches are not therapists and that I was not trained to heal my clients; however, if she was willing to focus on the future, I was interested in working with her. I stated that in her executive position she had to speak and act like an executive rather than like the nice girl next door.

At length we discussed the negative impact that her low self-esteem and timidity was having on individual employee performance, the organization at large, and herself. I learned that one person had vehemently told Lindsey what she would do and not do on the job, that another had openly disrespected her, and that the business simply was spinning its wheels. Staff meetings dragged on for hours with few if any conclusions reached. Because they didn't honor her time, folks expected her to be available to them whenever they appeared at her office door, so Lindsey ended up working most weekends. She wasn't getting enough relaxation, and was experiencing a fatigue that wouldn't go away. She also felt small, inept, weak. This made her squirm.

From the outset I leveled with her about what I thought was going on and what I knew needed to happen. First, I told her I believed she was trapped in the cycle of abuse. Second, I pointed out that the repercussions from this abuse were taking a toll on her personally as well as on her organization. Last, I reminded her that as long as her company existed, she was responsible for its health and growth. Sooner or later she had to shed her victim identity. Nearly weeping, Lindsey asked me to help her develop—or reclaim—her voice.

Early on I discovered that Lindsey lacked clarity about the characteristics and categories of verbal abuse. While she had endured some sexual debasement as an adult, she had also experienced decades of verbal abuse in various forms. As I named and described these forms during a coaching call, I realized that before we had started working together she hadn't recognized a number of them for what they were— abuse. She assumed that minimizing her needs, invalidating her views, and accentuating her shortcomings were typical male behaviors. The education I provided opened her eyes. My strategies for countering or halting such comments mid-stream showed her how to stand up for herself. Lindsey wasn't used to doing that. She was used to absorbing and tolerating whatever anyone dished out because she thought that was what mannered, professional people did. Over time she began to see this differently. But progress was slow.

From there we examined the beliefs she held about herself, her relationships, and her work. As I read the list, I noticed many that kept her and the company stuck. Although Lindsey wanted something different from what she had, underneath she didn't believe she deserved it. Her beliefs proved it. I taught her that whatever she held in her head determined her reality. Then I led her through the journey of reframing those self-defeating statements into beliefs that served her and held her accountable. I also told her that self-care included more than candlelight dinners, exercise workouts, and bubble baths. For Lindsey it involved consciously choosing the messages she allowed to circle around in her mind. As she took control of the destructive mental chatter, she felt ready to initiate several long-overdue, necessary conversations with both employees and community leaders. We role-played the scripts over the phone, and later reviewed the outcomes. I offered suggestions for future delivery enhancement here and there.

It's not surprising that Lindsey's decision to leave her husband was the catalyst for notable progress. Many months passed until she felt emotionally secure enough to take that big step. During coaching sessions we occasionally talked a little bit about her marriage, but we didn't dwell on it. Although I never said so, I guessed that a separation or divorce might be on the horizon. After Lindsey moved out of the house, she created a life of her own—by herself—for the very first time. It was that physical move that built (or restored) her confidence. Once she had some confidence under her belt, she acquired a leadership voice in certain situations. She began to see that her voice gave her a presence, positioning her to influence people in ways she never imagined. Although Lindsey needed to do more work, she was on the road to success if not yet at the destination.

Chapter 15

DO WHAT NEEDS TO BE DONE

For me, marriage to Don presented numerous opportunities to do what needed to be done: administering insulin shots, keeping doctor appointments, responding to crises, caring for wounds. These things had to happen whether timing and circumstances were convenient or not. As primary housekeeper, I assumed all responsibility for cooking, cleaning, and washing clothes. Because Don couldn't drive, for years I handled the shopping, too. In addition, there were emotional duties such as keeping him calm during crises, comforting him during troubling dreams, and assuring him I'd be okay after his death. I viewed these as spousal obligations to be fulfilled—burdens born of kindness toward a very sick man. It didn't matter whether I liked doing some of these things or not. It didn't matter whether I had enough energy. Don's stability and well-being depended on my carrying through with them. I didn't get a break unless I opted to take one.

By the time I showed up to launch the AIDS Project, I'd learned that life is rarely predictable or easy. In those first weeks I couldn't have guessed exactly what I'd need to do that would tax my intelligence, patience, or skill; I just knew, going forward, that tricky situations indeed would arise and I'd have to deal with them. One of those situations sprung up less than a year into the job. The volunteer nurse who helped facilitate the client support group began to develop inappropriately close relationships with several men who were HIV-positive. Somebody informed me that he'd actually seen her in a bar drinking alcoholic beverages with one of these men. He went on to tell me that she had expressed interest in becoming sexually involved with this person. Needless to say, I was deeply concerned. The behaviors described represented violations of the volunteer agreement she'd signed.

I discussed this problem with my supervisor. We agreed that automatic termination, tempting as it was for us, could cause serious negative repercussions. We needed to be careful. The nurse was a friend of one of the agency's board members. She held a decent job in the community and was highly vocal. To top it off, she'd applied for my position and hadn't gotten it. My boss and I worried that through her skewed perceptions, fueled by resentment, she'd misinterpret her dismissal as my way of eliminating the competition. Someone close to her had shared with me that she hoped I'd fail so she could rescue the program. Attempts to turn clients against me and against all formalized AIDS services were a real possibility. Determined to undermine my efforts, she sought to discredit me.

Still the fact remained: This particular volunteer had insatiable emotional needs that clouded her judgment. She crossed clearly defined lines. During several polite conversations she'd criticized my approach to the work, accusing me of being too detached from the human beings I served. When I told her that staying for the long haul required a delicate balance of genuine caring and decisive withdrawing every day, I watched her flinch. The nurse had a short-term view of things; I focused on future impact. For months I urged her to interact differently with clients until I saw that it wasn't going to happen.

Someone in my inner circle had once informed me that occasionally volunteers must be fired. The message registered, though I had not yet had to take such action. But the situation at hand pushed me to change this. Calmly, in a face-to-face meeting, I fired the nurse. As I referenced pages of documentation, I noticed tears sliding down her cheeks. She didn't contest those reasons. Over the course of the hour I felt empty; she felt sad. At the end, studying my face intently, she thanked me for doing what I thought I needed to do with great compassion. I discovered that termination was hard.

Getting into the jail to provide HIV/AIDS education to inmates took some courage and tenacity, too. The warden, interested in scheduling a conversation with me and a few of his key staff, returned my call four weeks after I'd started my job. He asked me to bring along my teaching certificate and proof of my Red Cross AIDS facilitator training. Before we hung up the phone, he cautioned me about discussing available drug treatments with incarcerated persons because the county didn't have the funds to pay for them and inmates constantly looked for opportunities to sue. I didn't comment.

Days later I attended an early meeting on prison property. It proved to be a test of my endurance. Within minutes the head nurse vehemently spoke out against AIDS education for the people in their charge. With a loud voice and not a little anger she communicated her concerns about all inmates demanding HIV tests as well as current antiretroviral medication if they were found to be infected. She believed my presence and my instruction would stir up trouble in the cellblocks. Further, she resisted having to do more work than the medical department already had on its plate. As I listened to her rant and rave, I observed the warden who sat quietly, his elbows on the table and his fingers laced. His face revealed nothing. I wondered what he was thinking.

When she finished complaining, he asked me to respond. He wanted me to explain the approach I planned to take with their population. Immediately seizing the opportunity, I assumed a leadership role in the dialogue. I proceeded to tell the attendees that I'd stress the importance of taking personal responsibility for one's behavior and the consequences of that behavior, and that I wouldn't ignite fires of discontent. I assured them that I preferred to be a neutral party who sided neither with prison management nor with inmates. Looking directly at the warden, I said that I wanted to work *with* them rather than against them. My professional credibility was on the line. The warden liked what he'd heard, but the nurse walked out of the room. After the door banged shut, the warden told me he thought perhaps I could do them a service. He requested copies of my credentials and a signed liability waiver. Of course their lawyer had to check me out, and a background check would be conducted for security reasons. I was okay with that. I left that morning feeling victorious. Prison inmates desperately needed

AIDS education, and I was going to provide it. I'd just been given the green light to do what I believed had to be done, even if the nurse wasn't on board.

Every leader—every day—must decide whether or not they will do what needs to be done or take the easy way out. It's all about ethics and values. Credible leaders follow their personal core values as well as their organization's values. For them, acting outside of those values is not an option. Aligning those two sets of values makes it fundamentally easier to deal with the tricky moral dilemmas, obvious or hidden, that challenge anyone in a leadership position anywhere in the world. Anticipating and preparing for dilemmas, even if they are rare, is wise. Actually defining them, navigating them, and managing them is smart. It takes courage to face dilemmas head on. Unlike problems that can be solved within a finite period of time, dilemmas are ongoing and messy. Multi-layered and unpleasant, they stick around or resurface when you're least expecting them.

Doing what needs to be done with dilemmas and other issues requires sound thinking and planning. Consider who is involved, the nature and intensity of the impact, and potential positive and negative consequences. Be willing to make unpopular choices. And after making those choices, trust that you'll receive adequate practical and emotional support. Get ready to be vulnerable, and accept that you might be wrong. All of this requires strength of character. Doing what needs to be done essentially requires a commitment to doing what is right. Let your conscience guide you. Listen, then act.

You and your organization benefit greatly whenever you choose to do what needs to be done. Those benefits, observable and obscure, can be short or long term—or both. Take a look at seven of them below:

Enforces rules or expectations.

One of your star employees has been leaving early without permission at least three days a week. Other staffers have noticed and resent it. You confront her privately, but the behavior doesn't change; she senses how much you need her. Despite her value to operations, you start the formal disciplinary process. In anger, out of the blue, she quits, and you are left with a workflow gap. Still, you know you needed to call her out.

Resolves a problem.

As president of a civic club, you hear complaints about your most influential committee chair who bypasses critical information in conversations with potential members. As a result, misunderstandings about the organizational mission exist. You need to address the issue. Fully aware that she seeks your position, you invite her to lunch. You praise the work she's doing well and remind her to include the missing piece. You say you're sure the omission has been an oversight. She accepts the feedback, smiling.

Taps your resources.

To your horror you inadvertently discover that someone in accounts receivable has embezzled a few thousand dollars. You believe you know who did it. Before taking action, you contact the company's legal counsel for advice. You summon your executive team for a closed-door session. You scrutinize six months' worth of spreadsheets, and you think carefully. To stop the crime and confront the culprit, you identify the human and technological resources available to you and set them to work.

Strengthens a service.

Due to the increased volume of product sales, you, as a manager, recognize the need for an additional full-time customer service representative. It's no secret that the vice president to whom you report is committed to achieving success on a lean budget. Over the course of a month you gather evidence relevant to proving your case. In a meeting with him you skillfully present the data that can change his mind. When he sees how adding a staffer can ultimately save the company money, he buys in to your recommendation.

Allows others to step up to the plate.

When you find out that your office receptionist has been in a car accident and won't be back for a week, you wonder how the mail will get sorted and the phones answered. Initially you consider hiring someone from a temp agency, but soon realize this is an ideal opportunity for other employees to experience life at the front desk firsthand. Covering one hour a day, each person helps relieve a difficult situation and learns something in the process.

Provides an alternative.

You are the chief executive of a large nonprofit, and your board chair has called the regular quarterly meeting to order. Folks are not in good humor, as the news of future government funding cuts was disseminated yesterday. You notice side conversations during the financial report. Irked by the distractions, yet understanding their concern, you let the treasurer finish. Rather than moving to the next agenda item, you immediately suggest that for a specified length of time the board members engage in open dialogue about the anticipated revenue deficit right then and there.

Grants peace of mind.

When you do what needs to be done, you might experience a certain amount of tension and strain. It's the price attached to right actions. But at the end of the day you get to enjoy a hard-won peace of mind. No one can take that from you. It is completely yours to hold in high esteem and celebrate.

How frequently have you done what really needs to be done during your leadership career? Cite the most recent example. What was the outcome? What prevents you from doing what needs to be done in certain situations?

Morgan requested a meeting with me when she finally decided to tackle her tendency to protect and retain underperforming, sometimes malicious employees who deserved to be shown the door. As we talked, she appeared to be more confident and assertive than many of my senior leader clients. Her strong, dominant personality, coupled with years of uninterrupted, diverse professional experiences, positioned her for decisive and swift action in nearly every facet of her job. But this wasn't happening across the board. I listened in amazement as she offered examples of underestimating weaknesses and minimizing deficiencies in several managers. Deeper into our conversation she conceded that while they respected her as their boss, a certain percentage of her staff feared and distrusted her. When I asked her to explain why, she told me that they found her to be guarded, distant, and cold.

Because of Morgan's insensitive demeanor, inapproachability, and hard-wired reluctance to cut staff cords, she had not been able to create a cohesive team. Curious about both behavioral factors, I pressed forward with a few strategic questions crafted to elicit answers that might provide clues. With a poker face she described the instability of being raised by an alcoholic, mentally ill parent; her struggles in two dysfunctional, downright toxic marriages; and the challenges associated with multiple health issues. Morgan had known various forms of rejection and abuse—and plenty of it. She was a survivor—resilient, capable, controlled, and hard.

As I got to know Morgan, I realized that her chronic fatigue resulted from extremely long hours week after week with no break. Without mincing words, Morgan told me that she functioned on minimal sleep, historically took on a host of demanding projects, and participated in a few serious self-sabotaging behaviors. In addition, her board of directors, all too willing to let her captain the ship, offered little substantive support. I got the impression that she was putting one foot in front of the other just to keep going and not drop any balls.

Once we began working together, I detected significant fragility beneath that driven, tough exterior. This armadillo-like executive had feelings that she hesitated to acknowledge and own. I needed to explore them and appeal to them along with her stubborn insistence on excellence no matter the cost. I also needed to teach her how to show and leverage her emotions appropriately with others, especially staff, in a way that allowed people to see her humanity and feel her empathy.

When I asked her to describe how she typically displayed anger, she said she became quiet and rigid while boiling inside. She found it challenging to verbalize disappointment or rage in professional settings. During one coaching session in particular Morgan disclosed that she didn't manage relationships well in general. Regardless of the topic, in one-on-one conversations she rarely varied her voice tone. Others sometimes found that a bit unnerving. In meetings she had difficulty reading people when their faces were devoid of expression. Thus she was unsure about how to contribute to the dialogue in those situations.

Early on I assigned her a comprehensive leadership assessment designed to show us her areas of strength, areas to develop, and areas that might be interfering with her effectiveness. Morgan's results indicated a great deal of leadership competence. However, the piece that jumped out at me right away was her ambivalence about exercising authority despite her confident, assertive demeanor. The report also showed that she had a tendency to be tentative and inconsistent with staff. This explained her often exhausting efforts to continue working with employees who simply were incapable of changing their beliefs, views, behaviors, and actions. Because she gave these folks too many chances to prove her wrong about them, both Morgan and her organization had paid a high price. When I mentioned this to her, she responded by saying that she didn't want to cause others pain. Knowing her background, I understood the origin of such a statement. As a coach, however, I thought it would be useful to examine each of the failed key staffers and then identify the commonalities among them. That exercise showed Morgan that she was inclined to attract and hire individuals who lacked self-awareness, good judgment, and solid character. The wrong players negatively impacted the team.

Based on what had come to light, I suggested that we review her hiring process and practices for positions of great responsibility. I taught her how to conduct behavioral interviews that gave candidates opportunities to talk about how they had dealt with specific real-life scenarios in previous jobs. We discussed the value of listening to her intuition. Further, I provided guidance for developing internal coaching plans for every staffer who reported to her. To make sure she understood how to write these documents, I required her to draft a sample for me to critique. Performance expectations, recommendations for growth, and corrective actions, if relevant, were included. This material served as the basis for annual evaluations. As Morgan gradually interjected the plans into agency culture, she saw they made it easier to hold people's feet to the fire and to terminate anyone who refused to cooperate with her individualized plan. I reminded Morgan that she wasn't paid to be a caretaker.

Over time Morgan made progress. She involved at least one other trusted employee in interviews with prospective hires as a means of setting up a mini-system of checks and balances. By enhancing her observation skills she perceived some red flags, preventing a couple of major mistakes. Her biggest discovery was realizing that to some extent she remains vulnerable to error. She found that hard to accept. I told her she must learn to be gentle with herself, more forgiving. I recommended that she restructure her days to accommodate more sleep, exercise, and relaxation, and that she regard personal time as sacred. I also asked for her commitment to reducing the amount of work that she took home for the sake of her mental and physical health. Months later I was pleased to receive an email in which Morgan informed me of an upcoming two-week vacation, leaving a capable staff behind.

Chapter 16

MANAGE TIME

I learned the value of time as I watched Don deteriorate and die. Every one of those 3,000 hours in his final four months had to count for something. Or at least I thought so. Time was our most valuable commodity, and it was running out. I didn't deliberate between washing the dinner dishes and sitting in the living room with him. It was a very simple decision. I put meal cleanup on hold so we could talk. For the rest of my life dirty dishes would be there, but Don wouldn't be around. In those days I didn't view time as a neutral resource. It was paradoxical that it was both my enemy and my friend. While I hated to see him suffer, I felt fortunate that he was still alive. Occasionally the passage of time frightened me because I knew what it implied: With each sunset Don's death and my widowhood drew nearer. Slowly but steadily, the grains of sand slipped through the hourglass. I longed to stop the clock.

Until I had to meet all of Don's growing needs in addition to maintaining my job at the hospital, I didn't really grasp the concept of time management. I simply kept a wall calendar in the kitchen noting personal appointments; that was it. Occasionally I jotted tasks or errands on a sticky note, especially if I anticipated an exceptionally busy day. In general, however, from the moment I got up in the morning until I crawled into bed at night I moved from one thing to the next without a conscious strategy. As Don became weaker and sicker, I sensed intuitively that something had to change. No longer was I able to complete the daily to-do list filed in my brain. At some point I concluded that I had to organize and arrange my time in such a way to ensure that the truly important things got done. Through trial and error I discovered what could wait for a day or two without our world crashing down around us. I didn't study some expert's fancy, sophisticated method outlined in a book; I just figured it out on my own. Rudimentary as it was, my makeshift process worked.

But once I arrived at the AIDS Project a few years later I saw that my basic time-management process wasn't going to be good enough. Now I needed to consider effectiveness, efficiency, and productivity as the package upon which my annual evaluations and community reputation would be based. This meant exercising calculated control over my time. Words like *priorities, schedules,* and *delegation*—perhaps merely lying dormant in the dictionary for me—had to take on new energy in the real world if I was to succeed.

Six months into the job I carried a daunting work load. People noticed and expressed concern. Several volunteers wondered how long I could ride the merry-go-round without falling off. Fully aware of the inherent duties and challenges of my work, my supervisor gently incorporated chats into staff meetings about aiming for moderate balance. She worried about my health under prolonged pressure. While I didn't obsess over the pressures, I knew that stretched rubber bands occasionally break. I also knew I'd never be *done* as long as I stayed in that position; that was just the way it was. Like many professionals I learned to live with those unsettling feelings that accompany incompleteness. Somewhere I realized that not being finished from lack of discipline is very different from planned delay of certain tasks. Prudent, decisive bumping, in fact, was a tactic I used regularly after I saw how it kept my head above water. Bundling soon became another—visiting clients in the morning, returning phone calls at lunch, and writing reports in the afternoon, for example, eliminated task-hopping and saved time. When I concentrated on one type of activity for an extended period, I felt less scattered. Completely focused, I was more present to the business at hand.

As I cultivated reasonable competence around managing my own time, I began to see value in assisting chronically and terminally ill clients with managing theirs. In those days the majority of people infected with HIV developed AIDS. Once they reached full-blown disease status, their life spans were limited. It wasn't unusual for me to meet a new client and then attend his or her funeral half a year later. As I thought about it, I believed their remaining time on Earth should not be wasted. During individual conversations as well as support group sessions I raised the subject with most everybody. With sensitivity, of course, I dared to ask the hard questions: How do you spend your days now? What do you want to do before you die? Is there something in particular that you hope to achieve or accomplish? What do you need to say to the folks who are important to you? What is your unfinished business, and what are you going to do about it? What is your legacy? As your case manager, how can I help you add meaning to whatever time you have left?

We discussed these matters openly, my clients and I. Despite the emotion involved, these dialogues often motivated folks to change how they viewed and spent time. In some cases people experienced a more peaceful death as a result of finally addressing troubling issues or presenting handmade gifts to those they loved. As I watched people take charge of their time even a little bit better than they had in the past, I felt honored to have played a role. I demonstrated leadership in an area I hadn't considered a specific challenge of the job.

As a leader, you must govern and structure your time if you want to succeed and stay sane. Teach others to do so, too. Own it or not, this is part of your responsibility. When you don't control your time, it controls you. It becomes a savage beast that stymies productivity and saps joy. Unless you are among a small minority of professionals for whom time management is not an issue, you know this is true. You know what it's like to miss deadlines, fail to keep promises, forget commitments. You know how it feels to read hundreds of emails a day, deal with endless distractions, and try to please everyone. You probably engage in multitasking, double-booking, and instant messaging. On top of it all, perhaps you are caring for an elderly parent, resolving an ongoing plumbing problem at home, or supporting a recently widowed friend. In short, you're running the hamster wheel called "super-woman boot camp" until you either get sick or burn out. It's a crazy way to live.

As soon as you take steps to tame your time, you reduce struggle and strain. Even tiny steps help. Make no mistake: In the modern world nobody escapes negative stress entirely. But you can decrease it by identifying your personal and professional priorities, building your calendar around them, and getting organized. How would things be different at work if you actually did this? In what ways would your performance improve? How would your attitude shift? How would your enhanced time-management skills impact the people around you? It's worth thinking about, isn't it? You may be amazed by a sudden uninhibited flow of creative juices or a renewed zest for your job. You can't put a price tag on those benefits. Make friends with time, and miracles happen. One of the best ways to cooperate with time is to practice any or all of the following strategies:

Visualize your day upon waking.

Before you get out of bed, know where you must start and where you want to end up. Picturing it before living it allows you to move through the day more smoothly. Get clear about the non-negotiables. Visualization is a power exercise.

Identify your top three priorities for the day.

You can do this in the morning, or in the evening for the next day. Everything else takes fourth and fifth place. Although you might feel like you must complete a dozen things on any given day, start with the essential three and see where it takes you.

Center yourself at the beginning of the workday.

Sit quietly in your workspace for five or ten minutes to ground your thoughts, feelings, and energy. A tense body and frazzled mind cannot focus.

Concentrate on one task at a time.

Studies show that attempting to do several things at once fries your brain circuitry. You delude yourself when you believe that you can talk on the phone, type an email message, and mouth instructions to a colleague standing in your office doorway all at the same time and be effective; you will invariably miss or skip something important.

Collect what you need before you start a project.

Jumping up and down to hunt resources, materials, and various documents throughout your work process creates a series of interruptions that kill valuable time. It's like baking a cake: locate and gather all of the ingredients, bowls, measuring spoons, and pans first.

Categorize your tasks and block your time.

Make a list of all of your job-related tasks, then put them into buckets such as supervision, board, planning, marketing, sales, and administrative duties. Set aside two days per month for individual staff and team meetings. Whenever possible, reserve the same time block each day for sending and answering emails, making phone calls, checking social media posts, and typing formal correspondence.

Identify *the* single decision or action that can guarantee fast results.

Cut to the chase. Don't get lost in your list of to-dos. Identify the outcome you want most by close of business today, and set the wheels in motion. If you're honest, you know what you need to do. So do it.

Tackle your biggest challenge during your best time of day.

If you are a morning person, do your most difficult task before noon. You are physically and mentally programmed to handle it best then. It doesn't make sense to plod through a tough project in your off hours. When you do that the job seems harder.

Delegate tasks to others.

Regardless of your assumption, you don't need to do everything yourself. Assign certain tasks to people who have enough skill and experience to handle them. This is a win for you and for them. You lighten your load while they stretch and grow.

Manage interruptions.

Modify your open-door policy to allow yourself time to tackle your own work. Screen phone calls, and deactivate the email notification ringer on your computer. Tell people to interrupt you only if an emergency occurs during a designated one-hour time period each day.

Reserve the center of your workspace for your most pressing priorities.

Limit this space to accommodate three or four items that demand your prompt attention. A cluttered desk, especially the area directly in front of you, confuses your field of vision and sets you up for missing a critical issue you must address.

Establish a meaningful filing system and use it.

Create or adopt a system that serves *you* no matter what others recommend. Avoid messy piles on your desk, bookshelves, and conference table by filing reports, documents, and correspondence regularly. You might have to try several systems before you find one that truly works.

Schedule thirty minutes of weekly vision time into your calendar.

This is the strategy most leaders ignore. Yet setting aside thirty minutes every Friday morning to set goals for next week, next month, or next year can save precious time. When you have a vision and clear direction, you are less likely to be thrown off track. Derailment costs time and money for you and the organization at large.

> Do you know precisely where your time goes in any given week? How do you typically waste time at work? Why do you allow this to happen and continue? Which of the above time-saving tips are you willing to implement now?

I'd known Teresa for about a year before she expressed interest in working with me. When we actually sat down and discussed her desired coaching outcomes, I saw physical evidence of how overwhelmed she was: lusterless eyes, shallow breaths, rapid speech, and too many extra pounds. The owner of a successful small business, for years Teresa had been juggling an excessively full plate of professional responsibilities with that of coordinating her elderly parents' care on a daily basis. Watching her mother and father deteriorate and become people she no longer knew drained her emotionally. As someone whose world revolved around nonstop, first-rate performance, she was wearing out. Having no definitive idea of her parents' life expectancies, she understood that something had to change. No question about it; Theresa needed to lasso and structure her time, not just consume it.

Although she never referred to herself as a workaholic, I believed the term applied to her. She told me she averaged seventy hours per week in her business, resented having to prepare meals, and got little sleep. On the other hand she said she felt tired and anxious most days. Her health was suffering. Aside from a yearly vacation she had rarely taken time for herself. In the midst of trying to do too much, she was grateful for being able to hold things together enough to deliver her product, satisfy customers, and not fall apart. Further, interruptions seemed to be the bane of her existence. Teresa found them to be not only nuisances, but also pins in her high-performance balloon. After taking phone calls from family, for example, she said she frequently lost her train of thought and forgot to do minor but necessary tasks. All of these factors combined fueled her lifelong simmering feelings of inadequacy.

Teresa openly admitted to contributing to this situation that had gotten out of hand. She and I both knew that her reluctance to set boundaries with loved ones and friends certainly played a role in her frenetic life. Her tendency to waste time by surfing the internet for breaking news stories or fascinating articles on topics of interest also blocked productivity. Her inability to decline invitations to serve on various committees affiliated with community and professional organizations made matters worse. Somewhat embarrassed, she informed me that she typically logged a minimum of twenty-five volunteer hours every month. Teresa needed to prove to herself that she was indeed giving back and contributing to the world outside of her business.

The coaching engagement began with a values clarification exercise and a personality test. When I discovered that integrity placed first among Teresa's intrinsic core values, I pointed out that under the current circumstances she was out of alignment with the principle she claimed to hold most dear. I explained that while she demonstrated pristine integrity with her customers, she wasn't living in integrity with herself. Instead she was compromising her general physical, mental, and emotional well-being. Moreover, her predominant personality system popped up as a blend of performer, skeptic, and perfectionist. As I reviewed those results, I saw that failure to achieve goals, and inefficiency, triggered anger in someone such as Teresa. To decrease her stress caused by disorganization, I determined that she'd better get a handle on time.

During one of her coaching calls I walked her through a basic weekly time audit focusing on half-hour intervals to provide a picture of her reality. Then I asked her to identify her areas of professional genius and excellence, followed by areas of modest competence, and those of ineptitude. A light bulb switched on for both of us by the end of that activity—Teresa strongly disliked administrative duties such as recordkeeping, filing, billing, and troubleshooting computer snafus. Unfortunately she invested approximately 20 percent of her total monthly work time in tasks she regarded as chores. As a coach, I suddenly started to get very clear about how Teresa could find more time.

After only a few sessions I issued three recommendations that I viewed as essential to Teresa's process for managing her time. First, I advised her to create a schedule and stick to it. Obviously emergencies with her parents would occur and she'd need to take them in stride.

Otherwise, however, I expected her to honor her calendar and think of enticing incentives to do so. Second, I urged her to select volunteer opportunities more strategically. By that I meant that she should to some extent consider return on investment as such activities related to her business. I also thought she ought to stop taking on new commitments unless there was a valid reason. Finally, I explicitly told her to outsource secretarial, accounting, and administrative functions to folks who specialized in them. She needed to devote more time and energy to her areas of passion and skill. This would relieve pressure and give her greater fulfillment.

As Teresa implemented these recommendations over several months, she realized that respecting her schedule challenged her most. Still she occasionally surrendered to people's demands to drop what she was doing and meet their need of the moment. I cautioned her about being too accessible and quick to take on others' crises, which were frequently exaggerated or invented. I also insisted that she carve out sixty minutes each day to recharge, regroup, and refresh. At the beginning of her coaching calls I held her accountable by inquiring about those sacred hours. Eventually Teresa looked forward to them as gifts to herself. With pleasure she shared her progress in prioritizing tasks, reigning in over-delivery to customers, and letting go of some of the things she resented. She revised her evening ritual to include healthier snacks, a book to read, and an earlier bedtime. I was very pleased.

Chapter 17

TRANSCEND PERSONAL LIMITATIONS

When I was a junior in college my mother's health took a turn for the worse. Even on weekends and during the summers—away from her teaching job—she got remarkably tired. She was in her late forties; I was twenty. But I noticed and worried. Doctors, having learned of her bout with rheumatic fever in her youth, said the problem was her heart. Over time they detected a progressing, irreversible weakness destined to lead to cardiac failure. On occasion I watched my mother slowly climb the stairs to our front porch or to the second floor in our house, her body bent at the middle and her face pale. When she thought I wasn't look-ing, I caught her holding her chest until some sort of abnormal incident passed. Although neither I nor my three younger siblings knew all the details, we observed significant changes in the woman we called Mom. As a firstborn prone to taking on more responsibility than should have been mine, unconsciously I began to absorb her pain. In retrospect, my feelings surpassed natural empathy. Though I didn't get sick from it, I became very sad. That sorrow, which I hid, did not lift until a year after she died. I was only twenty-three.

I carried that tendency to absorb others' suffering into my marriage. Sharing Don's plight of going blind, losing major organ function, and facing death exacerbated this inclination. Insomnia emerged as its most burdensome, draining manifestation. Since childhood I'd needed eight hours of uninterrupted sleep. The chronic sleeplessness I endured over those two years most likely triggered the circumstantial depression that eventually became a secret, unwelcome companion. To the world I appeared thin, but healthy, composed, and strong. I went to work despite a succession of hellish nights. I cooked meals and cleaned and shopped, albeit ready to drop. I wrote letters and entertained friends. Desperate to order the chaos, I wasn't trying to impress anybody; I was struggling to survive. Out of sheer will I rose above the clutches of insomnolence. It was hard.

Of course my involvement with clients of the AIDS Project also tested my tendency to absorb others' suffering. There, however, I regulated it more successfully than at home. I wasn't married to my clients, and I didn't live with them. Though I cared deeply for all, I found it easier to detach periodically from their psychic pain, practical needs, and emotional ups and downs. But I never unplugged from Don's story. I didn't take vacations or carefree days off. Within the confines of our apartment's four rooms, pregnant with illness and distress, I couldn't relax. Short of covering my eyes and ears and flushing out my brain, I realized the impossibility of full mental decompression. Case-managing Don had no built-in breaks. Case-managing clients gave me some control over when I met with them, spoke to them, or did something for them. When we parted, I didn't go with them. Our lives were separate.

Other personal limitations soon came to light in this professional setting. Nagging self-doubt about my ability to create a multifaceted, highly visible program under community scrutiny crept in shortly after I accepted the job. While I didn't discuss it, I felt its presence. I also knew the origin of my skepticism. I'd grown up in a family that viewed the world as a scary place filled with lots of unscrupulous people. My parents in particular engaged in conversations about their own professional experiences that imparted negative messages that stuck. By the time I'd graduated from high school I already believed that I wasn't a princess, that my opportunities were slim, and that I could accomplish only certain things. I was quite clear about those things, and running a human service program wasn't on the list. To do the job I had to disregard much of what I'd heard and learned while under the age of eighteen. I had to create new mental messages.

My hesitation to offend, upset, or ruffle feathers was a limitation I needed to confront on and off throughout my five-year affiliation with such a controversial program. Its very existence annoyed and outraged more than a few people. Frank, graphic discussions about HIV prevention methods threw gasoline on the fire, depending on the group. In the early 1990s a young mortician invited me to be the speaker at one of the monthly breakfast meetings for county funeral directors. When I arrived at the restaurant, I sensed tension. I was there not because these middle-aged and elderly men wanted me to talk about HIV/AIDS, but because the new kid in their circle thought it was vitally important. In my presentation I was supposed to underscore the necessity of using currently accepted precautions while they drained bodily fluids from cadavers. As I talked, I noted an eerie silence as the men crossed and uncrossed their arms. I expected pointed questions to follow. It's not surprising that those questions came wrapped in anger and fear. A couple of these licensed professionals accused me of upsetting their business lives. Preferring to work barehanded, they informed me that they hadn't worn gloves in the past and resented my instruction to do so now. Dialogue escalated in both tone and volume. The harder they pressed, the more I sweated. At the end several men left without saying good-bye. Clearly I'd pinched a nerve.

Harsh criticism, particularly if I thought I didn't deserve it, was difficult to bear. I had a tendency to internalize and personalize it. Living with a perfectionistic, fault-finding father, who judged his children's actions with considerable bite, likely birthed this limitation. Nonetheless I was responsible for dealing with it. In my work at the AIDS Project I had a lot of practice. There was some humor in that, but also much pain. Criticism from people who represented various social sectors came my way in a number of forms: negative, destructive, practical, critical, passive, constructive, speculative, religious, and moral. Until I got involved in this arena I never knew how many different kinds of criticism existed. Strangely enough, while I didn't like it, I got used to it.

Every leader, regardless of education, credentials, skill set, and experience, has personal limitations. Quite simply, refuting this premise is choosing to live in denial. Great leaders cannot afford denial for longer than a few minutes or maybe a few hours. Limitations can be hard-wired in your personality or learned by observing certain behaviors in adults who were influential in your childhood. Your birth order can play a role, too. Stunted self-esteem and lack of confidence can be root causes of personal limitations, as can abuse of your body through the ingestion of illegal or prescription drugs, consumption of alcoholic beverages, and generally poor health habits. Whatever the source of *your* limitations, know that they impact your job and career as well as your employees, your volunteers, and your organization. Everything is connected; silos and file folders exist only in your mind.

Facing your limitations and rising above them requires severe honesty. It also requires a helicopter view of YOU—a willingness to examine yourself from numerous, perhaps awkward angles. It necessitates laying aside old tapes that still play in your head—those recordings of family members and others telling you that you can't be or do certain things. Real and perceived personal limitations have only as much power as you give them. Today is a good day to take stock of the following list of personal limitations and their negative consequences. Identify the ones that resonate most with you. Make a plan for managing them.

Fraud syndrome

Many leaders feel inferior to other professionals. Fearing that you are not as intelligent, clever, savvy, and wise as your boss and peers, you dread being found out. If you harbor this secret concern, you probably play small. Focusing on your accomplishments can be one antidote for this problem.

Perfectionism

Waiting to complete projects until you pronounce them perfect exasperates others and slows work progress. Declining appropriate opportunities for yourself or your organization until you acquire the perfect skill to embrace them hinders career and company growth. Know this: You cannot achieve perfection in anything. It isn't possible. Choose to say "done" sooner, and let yourself stretch for the sake of the greater good.

Overreaction

By its nature, life is an emotional experience. Occasionally, though, we overdo it. Not every work situation requires a strong emotional reaction. Blowing things out of proportion saps energy and mars your professional image. Crying about those two hundred emails sitting in your inbox or allowing an empty printer ink cartridge to ruin your day is irrational. Identify the people and circumstances that push your buttons, and plan a neutral response in advance.

Weak leadership voice

A high percentage of women leaders, and some male ones, speak with little or no authority. This shows up as timidity, soft volume, or verbosity when communicating a simple idea. It can come in the form of making statements that sound like questions, apologizing for delivering expectations to staff and volunteers, or agreement with your board chairperson over something you can't support. Learn to speak clearly, succinctly, and potently, with authenticity and ease.

Inclination to hide

When you choose to remain invisible and silent, you can't influence the folks you are charged to lead to the extent you're being paid to do so. Further, you won't impact company vision in a powerful way. Come out from behind your computer. Develop a presence. Take a stand. Be vocal and visible. Today women leaders especially should let themselves shine!

Reluctance to act

Good intentions don't make great leaders. Right actions taken for the right reasons do. Actions create movement in processes, procedures, relationships, and employee performance. That movement affects the bottom line. Hoping your staff members and volunteers who show promise will reach their full potentials isn't the same as devising a plan that ensures they will. Pick out one strategic action that you've put on the back burner and schedule it in your calendar now.

Lack of confidence

Low confidence is the number one success-buster for so many leaders, especially women. This is sad. Behind those pretty smiles, professional clothes, and fast-paced strides often lie ugly self-doubts that churn incessantly inside their heads. Second-guessing decisions, stalling big projects, and supporting the status quo are examples of confidence on the rocks. It's time to tune out that sabotaging mental chatter. Trying something new can give you the self-assurance you've never had before.

Exaggeration of facts

Overstating the truth, which is a borderline character defect, detracts from your leadership credibility. Blowing things out of proportion can come back to haunt you both short and long term. Get in the habit of discussing issues for what they are. If you don't, after a while people won't believe you. Practice sticking to the official facts when you tell your next story.

Resistance to networking

Holding the belief that you cannot network effectively with other professionals is a personal limitation. Refusing to network, whether at your workplace or outside of it, sets you up for isolation that eventually stagnates your job success and your entire career. Prolonged disconnection from people who can provide support to you and your organization is a big mistake. Plug one networking function into your calendar each month to ease into it.

Fear of failure

All people fear failure to some extent. Confining yourself to a familiar box allows you to feel safe, but such behavior stunts growth as well as deprives colleagues, clients, and employees of the best of you. Identify three individual and organizational benefits to poking your head out of that box.

Health challenges

The majority of people in leadership positions suffer from some kind of physical, mental, or emotional challenge. Heart disease, diabetes, and depression abound. Left unmanaged these conditions can erode job performance and mar your image. Be sure to seek appropriate health care on a regular basis, and get counseling when life overwhelms you.

> How do your top two limitations affect others in the professional environment? How can you manage these limitations? What step can you take today to begin that process? How would your job performance improve if you viewed your limitations as invitations for growth?

Did you download my free assessment entitled "How Is Your Loss Keeping You Stuck?" If you haven't done that yet, go to www.launchinglives.biz/pdfs/Bookassessment.pdf.

Phyllis was feeling strangled by her personal limitations when I met her several years ago at a cocktail party, but I didn't know it at the time. Her glittering blue eyes, bright smile, and fairy-like ability to work the room disguised her pervasive depression, low self-confidence, and fatigue. Intrigued by my business, she asked me to arrange a one-on-one meeting. I sensed more than a desire for an extended friendly chat.

Over breakfast a couple of weeks later Phyllis surprised me with her candor. Without delay she described herself as a sinking ship. Trying to do two jobs at once to avoid layoff from her company, she pushed through a brutal schedule while receiving almost no support from her boss. As an upper-level manager, a great deal of responsibility had always rested on her shoulders. She'd gotten used to that. Now, though, it was more than she could handle. She felt totally disorganized. Her decades-long tendency to let people dump on her had become a serious problem. To boot, her husband resented the extraordinary number of hours she spent at the office, on the road, and on the phone. He'd grown tired of the treadmill, and he made sure she knew it. His reaction to her workload added even more stress to her already tense life. Phyllis told me that she got very little sleep and didn't take time to eat during the day. Her stomach churned; her neck ached. When I inquired about alcohol intake, she said she'd recently started to drink in the evening just to calm down. She felt badly about that ritual and sincerely wanted to stop.

With no hesitation Phyllis recounted the highlights of her life: severe ongoing physical, sexual, and emotional abuse from family members that culminated in a diagnosed eating disorder. At the time I met her she'd been free of abuse and anorexia for quite a few years. But the scars remained. They took the form of sacrificing her health and personal plans for the sake of satisfying others' expectations and desires. They also showed up in her belief that no matter what she did she wouldn't be good enough, secure enough, or rich enough. Viewing life through the lens of lack, she doubted her ability to rise above the damage done in her turbulent past.

Despite years of therapy, Phyllis still didn't trust herself to make appropriate, smart major decisions. Further, she continued to fear rejection and failure, and often gave in to a loud inner critic. Since childhood she had disliked anger and any kind of confrontation, especially involving men. She'd grown accustomed to her adverse physical reactions when in the company of people with authority: queasiness, body quivers, and cracks in her high-pitched voice. Despite her age and position, she admitted to difficulty establishing eye contact with her boss. At the same time, however, she told me she nurtured a habit of building up bosses and massaging their egos so they'd feel positively toward her. The strength she historically demonstrated with colleagues and staff hadn't transferred to her interactions with those in supervisory roles. This was a constant source of frustration.

At the conclusion of our get-acquainted meeting I communicated several things to Phyllis. First, I recommended that she develop healthy self-love as a platform supporting all of her actions. Second, I advised her to map out the expenditure of her finite energy both at work and at home. Third, I pointed out that she had choices even when it appeared she didn't. I welcomed an opportunity to name and describe those choices for her and show her how to make them in a way that would benefit her as well as other people.

After Phyllis hired me, we conducted an analysis of her life as a whole. Through this exercise she learned that she was committed and loyal, generous and focused. She saw that she was too emotional and ambivalent, and easily hurt and controlled by extended family. As we discussed trends, she realized that for decades she'd been hypervigilant, overly responsible, and submissive. Her personality-system test revealed a perfectionist performer—someone who emphasized doing over being. Understanding that she linked her self-worth exclusively to service and productivity, I helped her identify her intrinsic value and the specific contributions she brought to various professional tables. Together we listed commitments Phyllis could make to herself and discussed potential blocks to honoring them. I also taught her how to initiate critical conversations with her employees, husband, parent, and boss. We incorporated role-play into several coaching sessions. I provided respectful but direct language suitable for each scenario, and required her to practice that language in front of the bathroom mirror or in the car before actually using it.

Unwilling to settle for more of the same, Phyllis slowly began to transcend the personal limitations that had dragged her down for so long. Stepping out of her comfort zone, she told her boss she needed a break, her mother to stay out of her business, and a staffer to clean up his act or get out. She let her husband know how he added to her stress, and she asked him to stop. She traded wine for tea after work, went to bed earlier, and booked a vacation. I was proud of her as I listened to more and more examples of her taking charge of her life. For the first time she was choosing to do things that brought her peace and joy. To my surprise she even considered leaving her job. Stay or go, I assured her I'd support her either way.

Chapter 18

REBOUND FROM SETBACKS

Looking back on it, my marriage to Don prepared me to survive and rebound from setbacks. His loss of vision despite state-of-the-art treatment for diabetic retinopathy—a mind-boggling complication for both of us—was the first. Others quickly followed: forced retirement, distancing of friends, and unexplained insulin shocks too numerous to count. By our third wedding anniversary I grasped that setbacks, large and small, defined our lives. I faced the choice of flee or cope. For me, leaving wasn't an option. I'd made my vows to stay and love in sickness and in health.

The experience I gained during those years provided a solid foundation for dealing with expected and unexpected setbacks in the AIDS Project. There were many of each. It seemed, however, that some of the most impactful setbacks occurred in the volunteer buddy system I'd initiated within four weeks of starting the job. Early in the game I recognized that clients infected with HIV probably could benefit from having someone in their life who willingly spent time with them, helped them reach their short-term goals, and genuinely cared about them. After I designed an application process, I placed advertisements in local papers to recruit people from the community to serve as buddies. The first match took place between a young businessman and a male client about his age.

After several folks made a commitment to the buddy system, I created a formal orientation program that included evening training in

HIV biological, medical, psychological, and social issues over a period of six weeks. These volunteers, needing to come to terms with their own eventual deaths, learned how to help clients handle their dying. A variety of guest experts and I provided this comprehensive education. It's not surprising that the buddies developed close bonds with each other throughout the interactive orientation. The uniqueness of their work drew them together.

Unfortunately not everyone stuck around when things got tough. Accepting the role of buddy resembled getting on a physical and emotional roller coaster with a person doomed to die. Each individual who came on board assumed he or she could weather client storms—until they actually hit. Occasionally these cloudbursts, often unpredictable and dramatic, weeded out a few people. When a buddy quit, his or her absence left a hole not only in a client's life but also in the group. It was my responsibility to plug the hole, and usually that didn't happen fast. The client felt betrayed by the volunteer and frustrated with me. Buddy detachments fell into the category of programmatic setbacks from which I had to recover.

The most significant setback occurred three years into a fully functioning program when the person I considered to be the volunteer leader betrayed me. It felt like a punch in the face. This was someone I'd trusted and held in high esteem. For a long time I'd relied on his ideas, savvy, and judgment. In fact, I'd viewed him as a partner regarding anything related to the buddy system. Rarely did I make decisions affecting any of the buddies without seeking his input. In many ways I'd found him to be intelligent, sensitive, and wise. When I realized what was going down, I nearly cried.

The treachery surfaced when Ted (not his real name), a key player in the project, contacted my supervisor on several occasions behind my back to warn her about problems he perceived and issues with me. My boss, who believed she was aware of all program aspects and nuances, told me she was stunned. During a private conversation she listed Ted's concerns. In short, he disliked my personality, style, and approach. He viewed me as unqualified to run the project and labeled me as an unprofessional, ivory-tower coordinator who couldn't relate to clients' messy lives. Without offering specifics he referenced communication breakdowns. He accused me of forcing buddies to fundraise and using them to do service-related dirty work. As a result of these complaints, Ted had decided to exit the program. He'd reconsider only if I was dismissed. As I listened, my cheeks burned from embarrassment and rage. I felt I was being framed, and had no idea what to do about it. Suspended in space, I sat like a robot, scrutinizing my boss's unreadable face.

There was a lot at stake: the future of the project, my reputation, the relationship with my supervisor, and my job. All of these were important to me. Further, I wondered why Ted had waited well over two years to lay his bitter cards on the table. I thought he held me in high esteem and that we were friends. This sudden whiplash caused me to doubt him.

My boss scheduled a meeting for the three of us. She had an obligation to explore Ted's grievances in greater detail, and she wanted me present. Three days later I watched in amazement as my volunteer leader articulately and civilly ripped me to shreds. He did it in earnest with no apology. At the end of the meeting he announced his intention to remain in the buddy program, informing us that now he was *healed*. I couldn't believe my ears. Smiling, he got up and left. If Ted had wanted an audience, he'd gotten one. My nerves were frayed.

Despite this fabricated drama, due diligence prompted my supervisor and me to attend the next buddy support meeting together to present a unified front. At that meeting we sensed a nondescript discontent among the growing band of sincere but emotionally driven volunteers that lay beneath Ted's venom. Perhaps I was being blamed for whatever hadn't jelled naturally for them in terms of intimate group dynamics. Regardless, we addressed the challenges and uncertainties associated with growth and assimilating new people into the mix. We assured them we'd help get them to the other side.

Two years later, after I resigned my position to move out of town, we learned that Ted had wanted my job. To get it he tried to ruin me. While his plan didn't work, his behavior had shocked and stressed me beyond words. My relationship with him was never the same. Yet the fiasco made me wiser. I didn't take people and situations at face value anymore. Instead I looked for the hidden, underlying, contaminated currents that within an instant could change everything.

Setbacks on the job happen to all leaders. It's not a matter of *if* they will occur; it's a matter of when and what and how. Setbacks, part of life, can feel like we're losing control. Although irritating and discouraging, they can be learning experiences for even the most seasoned professionals. By their nature they remove the cataracts from our eyes and let us see things we never saw before. They help us view and comprehend the bigger picture. If we're amenable, they can make us strong.

Setbacks come in various forms. Your star performer fails to complete a major project on time. A brand new hotshot product doesn't sell. Funding for a necessary service doesn't come through. An envious colleague betrays a confidence. A board member undermines your efforts. Somebody else lands the promotion you've wanted for years. These are just some examples of the kinds of setbacks people in leadership positions must endure and accept.

Dealing with setbacks requires flexibility, resilience, and perspective. It takes a certain amount of physical, mental, and emotional energy. Setbacks are a test of your character and will. When they dash your world, you can crumble or quit. Or you can pick yourself up and keep going. One way to do that is to enter what I call a neutral zone—the gap between joy and misery. View your current setback, awful as it may seem, as a fact that is neither positive nor negative, but just *is*. This radical mindset shift can influence the final outcome. Setbacks always bring challenge, but they don't have to bring defeat.

Smart leaders expect setbacks. Savvy leaders, upon regaining their equilibrium, look for the benefits to these threatening events. You might grow to be tougher and more tenacious. You might have an opportunity to expand your capacity for compassion. Perhaps you discover an innovative spirit you didn't know you had. Because of what you bear, you serve as a role model for others as you explore options for going around, over, or through the obstacle. You show people how to prosper despite the twist of fate, the roadblock, the dirty pool—and you have a story to share when the time is right. Success takes on new meaning.

Not sure how to rebound? An unknown author once wrote that breakdowns can create breakthroughs. My seven-step process below can facilitate this happening for you:

1. Acknowledge the setback.

Name it aloud. Don't pretend it doesn't exist by sticking your head in the sand or burying yourself in work. Let yourself feel the anger, help-lessness, and fear associated with the setback. Write freely about it in a journal. Don't hold back.

2. Talk about it.

Share the situation with a trusted colleague, partner, or friend in a safe environment. When someone listens with their whole being, some of the burden is lifted from your shoulders. Invite that person to pro-vide insights and possible solutions. Tell them you want to hear about their own experiences with setbacks and how they coped with them.

3. Avoid blame.

Though it's a natural response, blame doesn't change the situation. Because it can ruin relationships and deplete your energy, blame often makes things worse. Get honest and determine whether or not *you* played a role in the setback. If so, forgive yourself. If others played roles as well, additional forgiveness might be needed.

4. Look for the higher purpose.

What do you know now that you didn't know before you suffered the setback? Think about how you can use that new knowledge to your personal advantage and the advantage of your company or organiza-tion. Who are you being now? Perhaps, as a result of the situation, you need to lead in a different or unique way. While the Divine didn't give you the problem, a spiritual lesson might abide in it.

5. Revise your expectations.

Setbacks can show you where you expected too much in the first place from a person, group, product, process, or opportunity. As a leader, your job is to minimize the chances for setbacks to occur at all. Take off your rosy-colored glasses and look at everything around you the way it is. Identify your blind spots about favorite employees, an esteemed funder, outdated procedures, or a short timeframe. Face reality.

6. Take responsible action.

The best salve for setbacks is action. Refuse to be a victim who sulks in the corner. Review your resources and plan next steps based on the information you have now. Decide what ought to be done in light of current circumstances and who should be involved. Carefully examine your reasons. Responsible, honorable action is always rewarded. Just don't expect instant success.

7. Use humor.

Laughter always helps. Even a forced smile can elevate your mood. As endorphins increase in your brain, you are better able to tolerate disappointments and deal with stress. As your anxiety level goes down, your ability to solve problems goes up. Humor removes some of the heaviness associated with setbacks, creating room for hope. Occasionally give yourself permission to chuckle and joke. If you must, do it in secret.

> What has been your most recent setback? How did it impact you, personally, and your organization? What did you learn about yourself and business as a result of dealing with this setback?

Be sure to take advantage of my free assessment, "How Is Your Loss Keeping You Stuck?" I invite you to download it at www.launchinglives.biz/pdfs/Bookassessment.pdf.

A previous client referred Sarah to me six months after her husband committed suicide. He thought I might show her how to salvage the family business in the midst of deep grief. When I phoned Sarah to see how I could help, I realized I was talking to a woman still in shock. Fragile and afraid, she relayed to me details from the tragic event that had rocked her world, as well as the fallout from it, while I patiently listened.

In the aftermath of her husband's death Sarah didn't know where to start to pick up the pieces. Fortunately she wasn't stressed financially for the short term, but she worried a lot about the long term. Her grief turned to anger whenever she dared to face the dizzying fact that for the foreseeable future *she* had to bear all of the burdens at work and at home. There was no one to share the load. For her, being constantly overwhelmed was the running theme. It's not surprising that professional disorganization followed the personal chaos. Unable to focus, she wasted a lot of time in the office. A self-described jack rabbit, she hopped from one task to the next throughout her day with no defined goals. She kept losing things. Uncomfortable with conflict, she avoided difficult, potentially explosive conversations with family members and staff. Unfortunately some key clients left, and a vital employee threatened to quit. Accounting reports showed that monthly revenue had declined. The business was headed for trouble.

Sarah found it hard to ask for support. She decided to hire me primarily because she knew my story. She also knew she needed a confidential sounding board and guidance for earning a living for herself and her teenaged children. If the business failed, she had no idea what she'd do. She felt abandoned, lost, and terribly alone. Her pain was raw, her energy low. Ambition, once important to her, had disappeared. Eating and sleeping were hit and miss. Like a zombie she went through the motions of what she believed she was supposed to do without having any idea of what she wanted. She thought I could help her sort it out.

As a career development specialist who frequently serves executive women suffering from loss, I recommended a two-pronged approach to the coaching: deal with the grief and clean up the business—simultaneously. Through her tears Sarah expressed a readiness to begin. She realized she hadn't been able to accept her new life on her own. Until now she hadn't had to cope with major change. She welcomed the idea of having a partner trained to support her emotionally and move her forward professionally.

Within a couple of weeks I learned that while Sarah had a positive self-image, her moment-to-moment confidence had nosedived because of the trauma. Suddenly she viewed the world as a frightening place where failure occurred more commonly than success. In survival mode, she wasn't able to trust most other people, including a few hypercritical members of her family of origin. She couldn't envision taking charge, standing tall, and winning—at anything. I told her she could do it but that healing was a process that could not be rushed.

I outlined my strategies for the next several months according to the priorities I'd heard. Getting Sarah on a self-care regimen and teaching her how to cope with change was paramount. Establishing criteria for making decisions and setting goals came in second. Managing distractions was next, followed by dealing with the excessive clutter in her house and on her desk. If time allowed, we'd discuss the pros and cons of keeping and growing her business.

Understanding that physical well-being, one of her core values, played a significant role in her personal healing and her ability to maintain the business, Sarah resumed an exercise program she'd neglected for over a year. I urged her to see some friends she enjoyed to restore a sense of normalcy to her life on weekends. Unclear about who she was now or how she fit into others' expectations of her, she hesitated to socialize. During phone sessions I gently encouraged her to spend a couple of hours with familiar folks who weren't her kids.

On the work front Sarah took steps toward greater productivity by dividing her days into chunks and putting effort into more tasks that truly utilized her competencies. I taught her how to handle interruptions without offending people, and I held her accountable. Together we created a list of goals and then triaged them, attaching a tentative timeframe for completion to each. Further, I strongly suggested that she stop trying to be everything to everybody and get clear about the *why* behind every action.

For Sarah, progress was inconsistent and slow. Intermittent insomnia, fatigue, and despair interfered. Nonetheless, the progress that did occur was real. We celebrated little victories like refusing to read emails the second they appeared on her computer screen, not taking all phone calls live, and not staying late in the office five nights a week. Other triumphs eventually came, too: ending conversations with a controlling male client at the first sign of verbal abuse, telling her parents she wasn't available to visit on an evening she'd made plans, and finding temporary happiness painting her nails and eating fine food.

The newfound confidence that resulted from honoring her needs positioned Sarah to stop avoiding certain things and make some decisions. She scheduled a long overdue appointment with her doctor. She cleaned out her husband's office and clothes closet. She remodeled a room in her house. A peacemaker at heart, Sarah told me in her final coaching session that she wanted to let go of the desire to keep everybody happy. She said it felt good just to say it. What really surprised me, though, was her decision to keep her business and speak openly about it to strangers at networking meetings. She looked forward to the opportunity.

When we parted, Sarah spoke less like a victim and more like a woman who'd walked through hell and survived. She was scarred, but she was strong. I reminded Sarah that her resilience, another one of her intrinsic values, was the ticket to her earthly security. She hadn't thought of it that way; she just knew she felt less fear. As she contemplated the future, she imagined bright possibilities, something she was unable to do when we met.

Chapter 19

ESTABLISH BOUNDARIES

About once a week during the final six months of his life Don became very demanding. He'd ask me to do certain tasks at inconvenient or impossible times: go to the grocery store for a single, unessential item; clip his fingernails; reschedule a haircut appointment. This was his way of taking charge of a situation that had gotten completely out of control. Typically he'd hammer away at his request until it got on my nerves. While he didn't intend to boss me, his voice tone resembled that of a parent speaking to a teen. I didn't like it. When I told him I'd do whatever it was he wanted later in the day or the next, his Pennsylvania Dutch temper flared. Then he'd pout. Occasionally the silence lasted for hours.

Boundaries weren't something I learned a lot about when I was growing up. My siblings and I hadn't seen evidence of them in my parents' relationship with each other. My father yelled at my mother in front of us using disparaging words; my mother carped constantly about my father's many faults. Further, my parents didn't engage in discussions about major expenditures; they simply went out and bought what they wanted. As a result of what I'd watched for twenty-two years before I left home, I realized I didn't know much about how to establish healthy boundaries with Don. I did the best I could, careful to avoid pouring gas on the already blazing flames.

Once in the AIDS Project coordinator's seat, I acquired more direct experience around instituting necessary boundaries with my clients and volunteers. The stakes were higher with them than with my husband, and positive and negative consequences existed with every new boundary I set. Shortly after I'd formed a support group for people who were infected with HIV, somebody showed up *high* to a meeting. Observing his slouch and dull eyes, inability to comprehend the dialogue, and ludicrous comments, I concluded that in the future no client would be admitted to these gatherings in such a state no matter how much he needed to be there. Illicit drug influence detracted from meeting purpose and productivity. I refused to tolerate it, and other clients shouldn't have had to put up with it. To everyone's astonishment, I sent the man home and explained why. With this decision I fully realized that he might choose not to return. But that didn't happen. He'd gotten the message, and two weeks later he came back.

When the buddy program kicked off, I immediately informed volunteers that they could not take their assigned clients to bars and could not, under any circumstances, drink alcoholic beverages with them in their homes. Stating what I hoped was obvious, I forbade them to supply drugs of any kind to program clients. Eventually I wrote it into the agreement they signed after my supervisor endorsed the suggested additional language. Enabling risky behaviors that could shorten people's life spans was cause for dismissal. My secret concern was that some buddies would view me as too strict or prudish, but I felt obligated to protect the well-being of the folks we served. Over the course of five years only one volunteer breached her contract in this respect.

The AIDS Project's discretionary fund, established through generous community donations and reserved for emergencies, proved to be an asset that required boundaries as more and more clients learned about it. As we drafted a formal policy, my boss and I identified specific criteria for spending these dollars: minor medical care needs, over-the-counter pharmaceutical products, housing security deposits, rental assistance, car repairs, and bus passes. Requests that fell outside of this scope of use had to be discussed. In addition, clients never received cash for any reason. My agency paid for certain things with checks, and buddies or I personally accompanied clients to purchase others. It wasn't long until several people asked me to cover the cost of luxuries such as hair color treatments and perms. A few women wanted their nails done. I even had a petition for jewelry. If the policy hadn't existed, things might have gotten out of hand. On any given day the most we had in the box was five or six hundred dollars. This money needed to go for essentials that impacted ability to thrive.

As the project expanded and client numbers grew, I determined boundaries related to the amount of time I devoted to each individual—and when. A year into the job I was forced to differentiate between client needs and client wants, as well as the urgency of each. Hospital visits to folks in serious condition came before routine checkup calls. Connecting someone with clinical depression to a mental health service by close of business superseded guiding a drop-in guest in locating the perfect HIV resource book. Talking with a newly diagnosed teenager and his mother took precedence over returning multiple phone messages from stable clients eager to hear my voice. In truth, many clients wanted much more of my time than I had to give. I found it difficult to choose one over another. But more often than not circumstances dictated who got my attention.

Other boundaries snapped into place on the fly. When a male client in crisis asked for my home address one evening, I declined. Right then and there I decided that my clientele must not have access to my apartment. I viewed inviting them into my personal living space as inappropriate and potentially dangerous. I set another boundary in an instant when a female client inquired about the details surrounding the domestic abuse suffered by her support group friend. Discussing one client's adversity with another broke the confidentiality ethics of my industry. Somewhere along the line I also decided that I wouldn't tell clients what to do unless I sensed they were on a very slippery slope. That was a different sort of boundary for me as a case manager—refraining from giving in to the temptation to play God. My job was to inform and guide, support and listen. At times I held people accountable for their actions or lack of action. That was all.

Boundaries, whether they are invisible lines or tangible barriers, define limits. They serve as guides. Responsible leaders set reasonable limits for themselves and others in their charge. In the workplace, clear boundaries send a signal to both employees and volunteers that certain things are expected to happen and other things should never happen. Leaders must establish boundaries for relationships, behaviors, work/ life balance, and performance. Communicating these boundaries and laying out the consequences for breaching them is essential. When weak or no boundaries exist or folks aren't clear about what they are, individuals and companies pay a price. That price can take the form of low morale and declining motivation, verbal abuse and physical violence, lying, cheating, bullying, and stealing. It can also involve legal liability. Or the cost can be more subtle, showing up as chronic exhaustion in people who are habitually overworked.

First and foremost, determining sensible boundaries requires your commitment to create and sustain a healthy environment. It requires you to prove your personal support of basic principles, regulations, and rules. Testing your strength of character, boundary-setting forces you to take responsibility for all aspects of organizational function. Of course you risk triggering others' anger. You'd be surprised if nobody got mad. Thus behind every boundary-setting process lies this critical question: To what extent are you willing to be a leader even when it's hard?

It's understandable that sometimes fear and guilt get in the way of boundaries. It's human nature to worry about people's reactions to lines that must be drawn. So how you present those lines can matter more than the boundaries themselves. Use diplomacy, but be firm. For example, don't apologize for informing folks that social media diversions must take place only over breaks and lunch, or raising one's voice with customers is completely forbidden. Explain the purpose of each boundary as well as measures of enforcement.

Take a look at ten personal and organizational benefits to boundaries below:

1. You foster a culture of respect.

When people actually know how you expect them to interact with each other and with you, they pay closer attention to their choice of words, voice volume and tone, and body language. They know you are listening and watching. High-quality interpersonal treatment among players at all levels impacts the bottom line in a positive way.

2. You protect people, their property, and their rights.

In most cases formal policies that prohibit abuse, harassment, and theft thwart these sorts of unwanted, unacceptable behaviors in the workplace. As a leader, part of your job is to keep folks safe. When people feel they don't have to be concerned about physical, sexual, or emotional harm, they can relax and focus on their work.

3. You uphold organizational standards.

The behavioral, productivity, and achievement standards by which you operate generally stem from the organization's mission, beliefs, and values. Specific performance standards are tied to employee job descriptions. Upholding standards compels everyone associated with your company to create and actualize attainable goals.

4. You increase efficiency.

When people work within clearly defined boundaries, they waste less time trying to figure out what they are to do and how they are to do it. They are already aware of your expectations in all of the important buckets. In this era of needing to accomplish more within the same amount of time, greater efficiency across the board counts.

5. You have a yardstick.

Once you set clear boundaries in any area, refer to them when some-body pushes up against them. Boundaries determine the code of conduct and behavior for your environment. In regard to performance, boundaries serve as indicators of whether or not people make the mark. Evaluating success becomes less subjective.

6. You provide structure.

Boundaries offer a framework in which employees and volunteers can do their jobs and interact with each other. This framework is the guidance all people need and expect in order to function at their best. It brings order to the natural chaos inherent in any organization or situation. Too many boundaries, however, can hinder creativity. Your challenge is to strike a balance.

7. You enable people to feel secure.

If you are a parent, you know that boundaries help children and teens feel safe. While they might rebel or resist temporarily, they generally appreciate these lines in the sand, especially in rough waters. Most human beings do not thrive in a sea of unlimited freedom because they can find it overwhelming. People prefer some invisible walls in which to operate.

8. You position folks to focus.

When staff and volunteers feel secure in the workplace, they are better able to focus on what they are to accomplish. They don't need to wonder if they are doing the right thing in the right way. Established boundaries provide guidance for the day-to-day *what* and *how*. This clarity increases engagement and diminishes stress.

9. You instill a sense of accountability.

Think of boundaries as benchmarks for behavior and performance. They provide the lens through which you and others view and assess the way staff and volunteers talk, act, and deliver. When people know they are being held accountable, they typically think twice before demeaning a colleague or slacking on the job.

10. You sharpen your assertiveness skills.

As soon as you make the decision to set any kind of boundary, you confidently declare your willingness to take a stand for something. The people in your world need to see you do this on a regular basis. As they watch you step into your power, they develop greater esteem for you as their leader. Whether they choose to be silent or vocal, they haven't missed your moves.

> What boundaries have you not yet set? Why are you resisting or avoiding establishing them? How can they resolve certain problems? What would motivate you to set these boundaries?

Because Karen had known me for a few years through a community business organization, she trusted me enough to help her improve her professional speaking skills in formal settings. Over lunch she confided that the company president felt she lacked authority and confidence during her presentations to small groups of potential clients in the conference room. According to him, she sounded too stilted and soft. Her smile artificial, she rarely gestured. Tired of Karen's timidity, obvious tension, and expressionless face, he'd agreed to cover the fees to have her coached.

A valued senior manager with significant longevity, Karen told me company leadership perceived her as knowledgeable, loyal, and competent. Despite the deficient public speaking ability, she doubted her job was in jeopardy. Still, she knew she had to clean up the problem area if she wanted to stay in good standing. Although her level of commitment was high, I sensed palpable uncertainty about whether she could do it.

A hard worker and a people pleaser, Karen basically liked her job. But she lived in fear. She often second-guessed her decisions and always assumed she was the one who was wrong in situations of conflict. Secretly she harbored a deep-rooted belief that sooner or later she wouldn't achieve organizational goals. I questioned her about the origin of this belief that regularly interrupted her sleep. She wasn't sure where it came from. Her marriage, loving and solid, helped her feel secure. No one appeared to be undermining Karen's self-esteem. Or were they? I was puzzled.

I began her six-month coaching contract by personally observing her deliver a two-minute presentation with key points written on an index card. As I studied her face, I noticed closed eyes, quivering lips, and a dry mouth. Her voice, apologetic and weak, fluctuated in pitch. I heard many ahs and ums. The content of the talk itself, while informative, lacked structure. At the end Karen looked embarrassed. She asked me for feedback.

Kindly I told her that we had a lot of work to do. I also communicated my strong belief in her ability to make the necessary shifts to position herself as a more credible company representative. Karen smiled faintly. I got up from the table and invited her to sit down. Then I proceeded to demonstrate body language, hand motions, and facial expressions conducive to creating a viable connection with an audience. I showed her how to stand tall, make eye contact, and draw people into the subject matter. I gave her samples of questions she could consider asking to increase engagement. When I finished, I explained why doing those things was so important. I mentioned reasons such as increasing personal authenticity, influence, and trust.

On several occasions over the next few months I required Karen to present a typical sales talk to me using the guidance I'd given her. I observed definite improvements. Although she appreciated my praise, she told me she hadn't extinguished the fear and intimidation she felt in the presence of men. It was real and relentless. She had no idea how to get around it. The self-confidence she'd enjoyed a decade ago was gone. Unclear about the direction to take at this juncture, I paid attention to a message from my intuition: Inquire about Karen's relationship with her immediate boss.

When I did, the floodgates opened. I listened as she relayed multiple accountings of insidious verbal abuse over the past four years. The most offensive was being called stupid in front of a group. I asked how Karen felt about this. Hesitating for a while, she finally said she didn't remember. To my moderate surprise she added that she was generally unaware of her emotions and had difficulty expressing her feelings. Beyond that she didn't think she *should* tell others how she felt about things. As a result she continued to accept scores and scores of snide remarks issued by the person to whom she reported. Choosing to keep the problem to herself, she tucked it in the back of her head and remained silent.

I informed Karen directly that she must set some boundaries around how her boss treated her. It was the only way to regain her self-respect. Nodding in agreement, she asked me how to do that without creating an adversarial relationship with him. I responded by saying that first I'd teach her the dozen forms of verbal abuse and have her identify the ones her boss commonly used during their interactions. At the time of our discussion about this issue, Karen thought that verbal abuse consisted mainly of put-downs and anger. She didn't realize that minimizing her concerns about a project or cutting her off on the phone were other types of abuse. As I provided more education, her eyes opened wide.

On one occasion Karen had told her boss how his comments made her feel, but he didn't care—or stop. So in the next coaching session I helped Karen write an outline of a conversation she'd initiate with the president of the company regarding her boss. We highlighted the main points and I advised her to describe the specific negative impact her boss's verbal treatment had on her job performance and personal confidence. I recommended that she stay away from words like *good* and *bad* and stick to the facts.

To prepare for this delicate conversation and emphasize her value, I guided Karen through an exercise to identify the strengths she had consistently brought to the organization as well as the major contributions she'd made over many years. We also examined the various voices available to her and together chose the best ones to employ in this situation. During subsequent sessions we role-played, with Karen being herself and me impersonating the company president. After much practice she felt comfortable calling the corporate office to schedule a meeting.

By the time a more secure Karen spoke to the president, she truly believed she was worthy of better treatment. Actually, she'd decided to leave if things didn't change. Fortunately her concerns were heard. The president offered to speak to her boss. While Karen never knew exactly what was said behind closed doors, she saw a difference in the man's behavior. She sensed his support during future presentations. This, along with all that I'd taught her, allowed her to shine in a way she never dreamed possible.

Chapter 20

MAXIMIZE VUCA

Living with Don resembled walking on an icy parking lot in high-heeled shoes or driving on a road surface covered with oil. I could anticipate some crises and detours, but certainly not all of them. On many occasions unwelcome surprises hit us out of left field. I could control some things and not others. The path was clear one day and cloudy the next. To use a U.S. Army term, I had to cope with VUCA: volatility, uncertainty, complexity, and ambiguity. For nearly eight years I did it on the home front.

When I went to work at the AIDS Project, I got more practice living with land mines. There VUCA showed up in different forms, the most fundamental being the unsettled funding situation for community-based AIDS programs in Pennsylvania. Beyond the first year of existence, The Department of Health made no promises. The state wouldn't guarantee ongoing federal financial support, and the program I headed relied primarily on money allocated by Washington, D.C. At several points during my tenure my boss and I sustained scares of contract cuts. During those moments I clearly remembered my initial fears of accepting a job with this type of threat attached to it. Later, as the executive director of a regional HIV/AIDS services planning body, I rode the roller coaster of funding uncertainty again. For another thirteen years I sat on the edge of my chair wondering if my organization would have sufficient dollars to retain enough staff to do everything expected of us. Somewhere along the line I got used to the hot seat. It became the ocean in which I swam.

Early in my employment in the field of HIV/AIDS I learned that clients lived chaotic lives. My job was to provide—or ensure the availability of—services in the midst of unpredictable circumstances. By its nature HIV infection alone created serious havoc. Because of minimal, inadequate drug therapy until the mid-1990s, people often received a diagnosis one week and planned their funerals the next. In the interim period most folks fought multiple, opportunistic infections, such as a rare type of pneumonia, skin diseases, and compromising viruses, that put them in the hospital for at least ten days. Painful and debilitating, many of these infections had lasting side effects. Even when completely resolved they sometimes returned with a vengeance within a matter of months. Thus clients' health status bounced up and down. That was "normal."

Add substance abuse, mental health issues, and/or a prison history, and the plot thickened. Most of my clients dealt with at least one of these. Except for a few, these people dwelled in poverty by anyone's standards. Social Security supplemental income coupled with food stamps barely paid for subsidized housing, bus tickets, and meals. Buying a carton of cigarettes threw off the monthly budget. For as long as I coordinated the program I never figured out how they managed to survive. The numbers didn't add up. Daily existence for them was a roller coaster that took all of their strength to ride.

I never forgot that my clients' chronic upheaval affected my boss and the agency at large. One person had a specific, unique need, and suddenly we were asked to create a new service, bend the rules, or work miracles to fill it. If we determined that we couldn't—or wouldn't—do what clients requested in certain cases, somebody paid a price. Over the years this sort of disruption took a toll. While I'd braced myself to endure the punches, I worried that my supervisor and the board of directors might tire of the emotional and reputation-damaging firestorms. At night I sat at home and wondered how long they'd tolerate the demands and threats issued by individuals whose fears drove them to plow through life like loose cannons. Naturally these thoughts increased my anxiety about my own job stability and program survival. But somewhere along the line I got smart. I concluded there was a vital lesson for me to learn in this: Either I'd make myself sick from endless apprehension or I'd face the VUCA and accept each day's challenges and trials. When I realized I was able to control only so much, I adopted a mindset of trust in my psychological strength and practical skills.

Today VUCA is everywhere. There is more volatility, uncertainty, complexity, and ambiguity than ever before in human history. Regardless of the industry, people in leadership roles can't escape it. Nor can they pretend it doesn't exist. If they do, individuals and organizations fail. Leaders must adapt and cope. One way or another they must make peace with the unknown. If they refuse—or cannot do it—they serve best by resigning. Organizations don't support leaders; leaders support organizations. VUCA weeds out leaders who want to coast. Count on it: The VUCA world demands a lot. But it presents opportunities, too.

To succeed, decide who you are *being* now in your leadership role and who you intend to be in six months or next year. Are you primarily being a decision-maker, problem-solver, or risk-taker? Are you being a facilitator, mentor, or coach? When you know the answers to these questions, most things fall into place. This is extremely important because it's nearly impossible to *do* if you don't know who you *are*. *Doing* aligns with *being*. After you determine who you are *being*, decide if you are working for a company that allows you to *be* who you believe you should be. If your company doesn't endorse your *being*, then find another employer. The mismatch doesn't mean you're on the payroll of a bad organization; it just means *you* won't prosper there.

Rowing the rapids of VUCA also forces you to look tough issues in the eye and see their relationship to the whole. It pushes you to rely on your common sense, years of experience, and collective skill set. It invites you to drink from the well of hope that reassures you that nothing stays the same and things will improve. Preplanned, positive mental messages enable you to walk into murky waters. Further, remember to manage the fears that clog your brain. Nurture a clear focus to stay on track. Self-discipline provides a solid foundation for embracing whatever comes your way. Stop fighting change and learn to welcome it. Resilience is your salvation.

Unsettling as your present environment may be, VUCA characteristics have distinct benefits that should not be minimized. Steering your ship through the fog allows you to set a credible example to your staff, board, and volunteers. People profit from watching you try unfamiliar strategies to suit unusual or extraordinary circumstances despite the fact that you can't see more than ten feet in front of you. They secretly applaud when you pick yourself up again after making a wrong turn or failing outright. It's exhilarating to realize that your courage, tenacity, and commitment to success can actually energize others to escalate their level of engagement. VUCA encourages you to shine. Not sure how to do that? Check out the following tips:

Give up your attachment to the past.

What happened last year ultimately doesn't matter. How you've implemented processes since the organization's inception is irrelevant. Historic strategies for supervising staff might not yield necessary results. How you made decisions just a few months ago could be obsolete. Clinging to the past won't serve you or others. It keeps you stuck. What will it take to move beyond the past?

Trust your instincts.

Listen to your intuition in every situation. Inner feelings, senses, and subtle nudges are important. Your head may interpret something one way, your gut another. In times of complexity and chaos consult more than your brain. Don't limit your depth of understanding by relying on intellect alone; you're more likely to make mistakes that way. What will it take for you to change direction when you know it's the right thing to do?

Create a culture of shared power.

Sharing power is not diminishing or relinquishing your power; it's a way to leverage it. Get clear about who you want to give power to and why, then assign those folks the authority to generate big ideas, make certain decisions, and lead complex projects. Organizations benefit from leadership diversity, and shared power boosts employee engagement. What will it take to manage your ego?

Teach leadership.

Invest time describing and discussing good leadership during individual conversations and team meetings. Let people know you think about it. Cite current examples. Because many folks want to be leaders at work, they expect you to develop your internal talent. By tapping their tool boxes you invite staff members and volunteers to showcase their skills and add different types of value as they grow. What will it take to make leadership development a top priority?

Embrace continuous learning.

It's not enough to develop others. *Commit* to expanding and fine-tuning your own skills rather than *resisting* it. Research options for learning how to inspire people, navigate difficult relationships, handle rapid change, and increase personal accountability. Make a plan and stick to it. Talk about it regularly. Sign up for webinars, read articles, attend conferences. What will it take to get *you* to the next performance level?

Build resilience.

To endure VUCA you need to build a firm foundation by taking care of yourself physically, emotionally, and spiritually. Eat nutritious food and get enough sleep. Pick an exercise regimen and work it. Meditate or pray. Schedule time to relax and have fun. Focus on past successes. You need a healthy body, mind, and spirit to recover from setbacks, adjust to change, and adapt to circumstances you didn't choose. What will it take to help you see this?

Develop a social support network.

Human beings are by nature social creatures. Further, in this complex world you cannot survive alone. As a leader, you won't do your best work when you're overly burdened by problems, disappointments, and fear. It's not a sign of weakness to turn to friends, family members, mentors, and peers for a listening ear. Their presence and advice provides a sense of belonging, security, and comfort. What will it take to reach out to someone you trust?

Ground yourself.

To get comfortable with turbulence, get grounded. Identify your rock and firmly plant your feet on it. With a quiet mind you can weather any storm. Take long walks, read inspiring books, meditate daily. Engaging in spiritual practices and rituals can help you find your center. When the next drama knocks, you don't need to freeze or fall. What will it take for you to position yourself to operate from your strengths?

Open up to possibility.

VUCA, scary as it seems, can be a gift. It invites you and your staff to go outside that familiar, established box and explore what else is possible. Shifting terrains, generally perceived as paralyzing threats, provide opportunities for innovation and creativity. They challenge you to stretch; to tap your untouched potential. What will it take to focus more on the stimulation than the fear?

Stay the course.

Your course is the organization's vision, mission, and strategic plan. Use this road map to identify priorities, make decisions, and take actions. Although detours might be necessary, clarify the *why* behind them before you leap. No matter what the temporary path, stay focused at all times on the desired destination. What will it take for you, your board, and your employees to do that?

> What evidence of VUCA are you seeing in your organization now? Until today how have you been dealing with chaos and change? How are you maximizing the VUCA landscape? Which tips from the list above do you intend to practice to manage VUCA more effectively?

Bonita hired me on a snowy morning to ensure a smooth transition into her new job as regional executive for a large, multilayered organization. Because I'd watched her confident, take-charge approach with community service activities for a decade, I was surprised by her admission to a masked fear of change. Over breakfast she said she felt silly doubting her ability to succeed in such an elevated professional position; however, those doubts loomed large, and she wanted to be transparent with me about them. Her eyes glistening with tears, she told me she usually didn't handle new situations with ease. She didn't think she could live with the shame that accompanies failure.

I soon learned that Bonita was the eldest adult child of an alcoholic. As I got to know her on a deeper level, I realized she demonstrated several of the characteristics typically found in this population: a tendency to judge herself harshly, the inclination to assume too much responsibility, the need for people's praise and approval, a disposition to overreact to uncertainties, the compulsion to control, and rigidity. During our first session I made notes about her putting in excessively long hours at work, running a frenetic pace, sacrificing family time, and rarely having fun. Underneath that very attractive, bubbly, energetic personality lay a lot of insecurity and resentment.

As expected, test results indicated that Bonita was a high-achiever as well as a protector of self and others. She buried herself in movement and hid from vulnerability. Unwilling to tolerate her own mistakes, she often held herself to unrealistic standards. But she used a different measuring stick for subordinates' behavior, causing her to refrain from initiating necessary, long-overdue disciplinary procedures. Observant, yet choosing to stand on the sidelines, she permitted a couple of subordinates to continue down the path of dysfunction. With embarrassment Bonita recognized how her inaction negatively impacted the organization in serious ways. She fully understood that refusing to hold key people's feet to the fire would undermine her executive efforts.

When I heard that her corporate office expected all satellites to begin a process of shifting operational priorities, I recommended that our coaching focus mainly on developing her leadership strategies and personal coping skills for navigating change and prolonged uncertainty. I thought we needed to concentrate in three areas: enhancing her self-awareness and social awareness, strengthening important relationships, and broadening her influence. I explained that by making advancements in these areas, she and her staff could face—and flow with—anything. Bonita saw the value of my proposal.

Upon completing an emotional intelligence assessment, Bonita discovered that she lacked clarity around her natural gifts, talents, and skills—as well as her stress triggers. She also noticed that she was able to identify her personal feelings in some situations but not in others. She saw that a myriad of distractions prevented her from being fully present in the moment too much of the time, and that frequently she either disregarded or didn't know how to respond to others' verbal messages and body language. Committed to remaining in the role of coach rather than stepping into the therapeutic domain, I briefly explained that her childhood focus of caring for an alcoholic parent intercepted her ability to connect with her own emotions and view them as separate from someone else's. It also fostered her mistrust in accurately interpreting the words and signals expressed by the people around her. Bonita and I discussed strategies that would help her close the gap in these paucities.

Because she described herself as fast-paced and high-strung under normal conditions, I presumed that large doses of uncertainty and ambiguity exacerbated her typical demeanor. Focused deep-breathing exercises, and mindfulness of opportunities to use humor, gave her some on-the-spot options for achieving a state of calm when circumstances got rough. I reminded her that since humor and inner peace represented two of her intrinsic values, she could serve herself and others well by proactively looking for ways to add levity and tranquility to stressful situations. To Bonita's surprise I boldly suggested that she train herself to embrace planned and unplanned change with a spirit of curiosity rather than fear. That was a novel idea.

Eventually I showed Bonita how longer periods of personal centeredness could reduce her propensity to speak to staff in a clipped, painfully direct manner. I felt confident that as she consciously revised her communication style, her relationships with vital employees would blossom and grow. Bonita did not have a poor relationship with any of the folks in her organization when we worked together, but I pointed out that her professional success and that of her colleagues depended upon a strong mutual trust that did not yet seem to have been established. Empathy, I said, was the cornerstone of such trust. She needed to talk to employees at all levels with a voice and face that illustrated her interest in and concern for each one. Her staff had to feel valued and heard before they boarded her bus. In preparation for beginning the challenging job of altering the culture, she needed to find out how they viewed things. Only then could she influence them to accept her vision, her goals, her processes, her path.

After six months Bonita had built a robust framework for gradually moving the organization forward as the corporate office had dictated. Confident and secure, she'd cleaned house to create space for a higher-functioning core management team. she scheduled time to get to know these people so she could leverage their strengths. As she developed bigger flexibility muscles, she realized that she was better able to address problems and deal with dilemmas. Observing her honed competence, she relaxed enough to start planning a life with a little more balance. Preserving her marriage and being accessible to her children was extremely important to her. At least three evenings a week she ate dinner at home. She arranged dates with her husband, and visited friends. Above all, having fun positioned Bonita to thrive in her whirlwind VUCA world. I released her without concern.

Conclusion

Once I matured into a fully functioning adult, Don was not my only loss. His death prepared me to deal with other kinds of losses and taught me how to grieve and how to heal. Everything that happened before and immediately after his death served as a training ground, or boot camp. As Don bore his downward spiral, neither he nor I ever imagined the losses I would experience during the next three decades. Little did we guess that a platter filled with disappointments, unrealized dreams, and sorrows waited for me. Had I realized that then, I might have frozen with fear. I might have made different choices, deciding to play it safe. I might have run or hid—I'm not sure what I would have done.

But I believe there is something to be said for not knowing the future. The *not knowing* fuels us to move forward with joyful anticipation, or at least reasonable curiosity. The not knowing provides the blank canvas on which we can paint the next picture—the blank page on which we can write the next chapter of our lives. The not knowing gives us the freedom to explore and stretch without the paralysis that often results from being indescribably afraid. It grants us the courage to become more than we thought we could.

One afternoon sometime during my first few months in the HIV field, a nurse-practitioner on staff at my community health agency stopped me in the hall. Catching me off guard, she politely but directly asked how a hospital business-office clerk turns into a coordinator of AIDS services virtually overnight. It was a fair question, and she was serious. By the look on her face I saw that she expected a rational answer. While others might have been thinking about this question, nobody else in the workplace had raised the issue with me. A long thirty seconds passed in silence. As I formulated my words, I considered the fact that she had served as a nurse in Vietnam combat zones, an ordeal that had totally changed her. So I told her that although I had not survived a war like she had, I had walked on a bed of nails until my feet and nerves were raw. Once on the other side I was a different person: determined, confident, strong. I'd developed a boldness and fortitude and flexibility previously foreign to me. I knew how to do things I never suspected I'd do. My natural empathy had deepened. I believed that despite its coarseness, all of this had to have marketable value in the world—in my world, small as it was. After I'd healed, I felt intuitively positioned to lead people, an organization, a cause. For obvious reasons I guessed I'd end up in the field of diabetes. Instead I ended up in a strange, uncharted field I couldn't have planned. The time had come, I said, for me to transform my pain into service. My loss mustn't be wasted. As I spoke, the nurse studied my face. Surely, I assumed, someone with her background would understand. We never spoke of this again.

What I didn't say in that conversation was that I'd acquired a sense of personal power I couldn't ignore during those years with Don. Like a fire it burned in my belly until I was ready to unleash and leverage it. I sensed I could do something big, something great, something very much needed. This wasn't my ego talking; the feeling came from the fibers of my being. I had to pay attention to it, and I had to figure out how to use it wisely. This required some serious discernment both prior to taking the HIV/AIDS job and then once I was in the seat. The discernment, of course, didn't stop there. Throughout my entire traditional career I engaged in that critical exercise, always looking for opportunities to grow people, influence policies, and expand programs. The more I tapped this resource to benefit a purpose higher than myself, the more of it I received. I never ran out of personal power, even when I thought I might.

That power, often elusive, kept me going as different storms of loss raged. In my thirties, competing candidates landed positions I sought. As I wallowed in defeat, I lost self-esteem. I wondered what those folks had that I lacked. When my infant nephew died from SIDS, I realized I'd lost the privilege of knowing him as a child and a man. As my brother's marriage fell apart after his son's death, I felt helpless and sad. Within months my brother became distant and rarely called. A few years later I doubted my femininity and lovability when someone with whom I yearned to tie the knot refused to make a commitment. Frustrated with his decision, I ended the affair. Alone again, I felt abandoned and lost. After my sister and brother-in-law resisted treatment options I recommended to address her debilitating and worsening clinical depression, I lost faith in my competence to help family members solve problems. As my sister shrank to a mere shadow of her youthful self, I recognized that I'd lost her as the person I once knew. In each case my loss triggered grief. I grieved all these experiences as a still relatively young woman. In the midst of it all I went to work, held my head up, and performed. Firsthand, over and over, I learned that grief is not a lifelong sentence. It's temporary unless *we* decide it's not.

Loss followed me into my forties, too. Near the beginning of a new marriage (after ten years of widowhood), without warning, I inherited from my aging father the medical, financial, and day-to-day oversight of my terminally ill uncle. Within six weeks of my uncle's death my dad suffered a major hemorrhagic stroke, topped off by seizures that permanently altered his health status. No longer did he walk without shuffling and appearing to lose his balance. Frequently he forgot what he was going to say mid-sentence. CT scans showed irreparable brain damage as well as a rare form of dementia. At some point I had no choice but to take his car keys away from him as a means of protecting him and others on the road. For the second time I assumed comprehensive power-of-attorney duties for a blood relative. Two more stroke episodes occurred, the last one confining him to a wheelchair and landing him in a skilled nursing facility for the next five years. I watched my father's physical and mental status decline, occasionally as if I were observing the process through a character in a play, and gave myself permission to escape for brief periods the harsh reality unfolding under my nose. It was a bitter pill to swallow.

The elder care that extended far beyond the life expectancy predictions for both of these people took a toll on my schedule, my relationships, and my health. During that period I was the executive director of a fourteen-county nonprofit organization with little time to spare. Aside from juggling the usual professional demands associated with my position, I shared responsibility with my husband for maintaining a large house. Driving to nursing homes for friendly, keep-my-thumb-on-the-pulse visits with my dad and meetings with care team staff during the workweek and on weekends swallowed up literally hundreds of hours each year. Finding gaps between obligatory appointments to liquidate financial assets at distant town banks in order to pay shockingly large bills posed a challenge. Being contacted during board meetings by doctors and nurses to make on-the-spot medical decisions over the phone wasn't always easy to explain to folks on the periphery. Getting calls from facility personnel at dinner while trying to catch up on conversation with my husband and wind down from a busy day sent my adrenaline rushing. Listening to my father, an hour away, cry about some real or perceived crisis at 8:00 PM typically delayed or interrupted my night's sleep. The once-familiar insomnia from an earlier life reared its ugly head. It's amazing that I ran this treadmill without breaking for over six years.

There were mornings after my shower when I looked in the bathroom mirror and wondered who I was. A tired face, enhanced by the magic of makeup, stared back at me. I experienced a number of perimenopausal symptoms: moderate mood swings, lingering fatigue, acne, weight gain. I preferred my body wrapped in a towel. I also preferred to stay at home on the couch every chance I got. I didn't have the energy to go out with friends. I stopped renewing magazines I used to enjoy. Actually, I just stopped everything except the essentials. In the summers we went on vacation, but I didn't relax. I pretended I was having a good time when really I was thinking about my uncle or my dad in the nursing home and how I wasn't as accessible to advocate for them should the need arise. Concerns for their safety and comfort were never far from my mind. By the time my father died in the fall of 2005, I entertained fantasies of somebody having to prop me up at the podium to deliver his eulogy. Exhaustion had become a constant companion.

When that time came I was emotionally at peace as I stood in front of seventy-five mourners. But physically I was a mess. Over 80 percent of my skin was covered in red and purple raised nodules that simultaneously itched and burned. I couldn't stand to wear clothing, sit on a chair, or lie naked in bed. Four weeks before the funeral I'd endured a freak exposure to a tarry sealant when a large section of the roof was replaced above my office suite. Quite possibly the ducts between the roof and the indoor ceiling hadn't been closed, allowing microscopic particles to rain on my body for four seemingly luxurious hours while I pushed paper, uninterrupted, at my desk that fateful afternoon. Nobody except my staff, a couple of colleagues, and a few close family members knew about this incident. Because the DNA in my cells had been altered, I spent seven years coping with various erupting health issues that sprang from that exposure, and learning to manage them. My immune system, abnormally hypersensitive, launched into overdrive, and hasn't stopped. Specialist physicians didn't guarantee any particular level of recovery or offer a timeframe for achieving stability. While I never missed a day of work, for months I lived in chronic fear of being unable to do my job as it needed to be done. The fear was a burden and a trap from which I had to escape.

In this calamity I bumped up against my own vulnerability in a brand new way. I wasn't vulnerable because I couldn't stop bad things from happening to someone else; I was vulnerable because of what was happening directly to me. I had lost control of my body. I had absolutely no say in how it responded to those toxic substances. My doctors felt powerless, too. For this woman—me, who appeared to others to be in total control and worked to create a life and career around carefully orchestrated plans—it seemed that this manifestation of no control might be the basis of my biggest leadership lesson yet. I thought there was a lesson for my employees, too. It was my duty to define and model it.

At the time of this writing I am aware of my middle-aged sister's impending death. Ironically free of clinical depression after a decade of darkness, the coronary artery irregularities and white-matter brain disease diagnosed more recently are bound to kill her. Slowly or catastrophically, it's going to happen. I don't know when; probably at a moment when I'm not thinking about it. Already she's suffered several small strokes and is losing cognitive function. Weak and tired, she spends most of her days in bed. She is saying good-bye to life. And standing in the wings sending sisterly love to her in New York, I weep silently. This is one more loss for me to accept. Though I am vulnerable as I watch and wait, I trust that I am strong. I remain secure in the knowledge that I am meant to go on and teach others, women leaders in particular, how to survive and transform losses. If we don't do this, part of us dies. Is that what you want?

YOU are not diminished or impoverished or pathetic because of your losses. You are capable and beautiful and strong. Whatever their form or intensity, your losses are gifts in disguise. They allow you to be and do for others what you could not be and do if they had not crashed or crept into your life. Your losses contribute to your uniqueness. I believe it's your duty to discover how this is true for you. I think it's your responsibility to find out how you can use your particular bouquet of losses to serve the world—to serve your staff, your volunteers, your board of directors, and your customers and clients. Losses are invitations to shine, not reasons to hide. That doesn't mean you must share all of the details, but you're wise to let people know you're human. This creates the bond without which you cannot build your platform or begin to make a difference.

Losses put heart into leadership. Yes, you can lead with your head—but only so far. People ultimately don't follow heads; they follow hearts. Don't minimize or waste your losses. Each one of them counts.

"From Loss to Light: A Blueprint for Rebuilding a Life That Works"

A Group Coaching Program

Is a recent loss—or an unresolved loss from the past—getting in the way of your ability to function effectively as a leader? Please keep reading….

Ever since I opened my coaching practice in 2008 I've noticed a significant, common theme among most of my clients. They are stuck in some type of grief that negatively impacts their work performance and overall quality of life. I'm talking about grief triggered by circumstances or significant life changes such as job terminations, illnesses or unwanted health conditions, marital discord, financial loss, divorce, death, substance abuse, aging, alterations in physical appearance, deteriorating elderly parents, mental health challenges, geographical moves, new jobs, and empty nest syndrome. Until this grief—past or present—either gets reconciled or resolved, it saps your energy, erodes your confidence, and kills your joy. Unreconciled and unresolved grief adds unnecessary stress, is exhausting on a number of levels, and holds you back from being all that you are meant to be. Sometimes people are grieving and don't even realize it. Could YOU be one of them? Is there a loss or life-changing event that you don't want to face? Or is there something you fully acknowledge but that consumes your thoughts and leaves you feeling incomplete because you can't get beyond it?

You don't need to resign yourself to an existence of simmering misery. **There is a way through it.** And that's precisely why I designed a twelve-week **group coaching program** entitled **"From Loss to Light: A Blueprint for Rebuilding a Life That Works."** As someone who has experienced many different kinds of losses during my life, I want you to understand that losses and grief don't need to hold you hostage. I want you to KNOW that the negative impact of loss can be managed, to BELIEVE that you can grow from your loss and use it to make meaningful contributions in your world, to FEEL that you can claim your personal power and hope in a happier future, and to CREATE a viable plan that moves you forward. How does this sound? What would it mean for you to embrace your loss and finally make peace with it? What would it be like for you to proactively create a different life that brings you more opportunity, happiness, and fulfillment? **In this group coaching program I show you how.**

This program is for YOU if:

- ✓ You suspect or know that your loss/grief is negatively impacting your work.
- ✓ You cannot concentrate and/or you experience memory problems on a regular basis.
- ✓ You have difficulty connecting with others.
- ✓ You feel chronically tired.
- ✓ You feel isolated and alone.
- ✓ You feel stuck in sadness, anger, and/or frustration.
- ✓ You sense that life is a constant struggle just to survive.
- ✓ You believe that life probably isn't going to offer you more than what you have now.

Program Benefits:

- Understand that the negative impact of your loss can be temporary.
- Receive individual and group support without judgment.
- Learn how to manage your emotions.
- Increase personal energy and motivation.

- Increase self-confidence and self-empowerment.
- Define who you are now because of the loss you experienced.
- Learn healthy coping strategies.
- Gain insights into how to grow from your loss and use your experience to serve others.
- Enrich every aspect of your life.
- Receive hope that motivates you to embrace your future.
- Create a viable plan for moving forward.
- Take steps to move forward in meaningful, creative ways.

Program Content:

This twelve-week program consists of the following:

- 6 one-hour telephone group coaching sessions (held bi-weekly)
- Exercises
- Email support
- Supporting materials and resources
- 1 half-hour private telephone coaching session with Sylvia
- Recordings of all group coaching phone sessions

Syllabus for **From Loss to Light** phone sessions:

- Phone Session #1:   **Defining and Understanding Your Loss**

- Phone Session #2:   **Experiencing Your Loss Physically, Emotionally, Mentally, and Spiritually**

- Phone Session #3:   **Changing Your Interpretation of Your Loss**

- Phone Session #4:   **Discovering Possibilities and Opportunities in Your Loss**

- Phone Session #5: **Recovering and Moving Forward**

- Phone Session #6: **Creating Your Personal Plan**

Why should you consider my program now?

You know you cannot afford to stay stuck because of your past or present loss(es). You cannot continue performing at a mediocre or sub-optimal level at work, isolating yourself from other people and failing to be emotionally available to those around you. On a soul level you realize you don't want to endure additional months or even years of feeling lost, detached, and miserable. Deep inside you absolutely believe there has to be more for you, but you don't know how to attract it and connect to it by yourself. The truth is that you don't need to figure it out and handle everything on your own. You can accept guidance and support from me and your program peers through this unique group-coaching opportunity designed just for YOU.

To learn more about this program, contact Sylvia Hepler at: sylvia@launchinglives.biz or call 717-761-5457.

About the Author

Sylvia Hepler, owner and president of Launching Lives, LLC, is a career development specialist for managers and executives. She supports clients as they upgrade their current job performance, seek a job promotion, or plan and navigate a career transition. Certified and trained by The Rescue Institute in Golden, Colorado, and Quantum Endeavors in Chicago, Illinois, she has participated in numerous continuing education opportunities with experts of national notoriety and participated in extensive private coaching for herself.

After earning a BS in education from Lebanon Valley College, Sylvia originally served as a public school teacher and reading specialist. Her professional background includes extensive nonprofit management and leadership, public speaking, HIV/AIDS community program start-up, HIV/AIDS program evaluation, business writing, and retail sales. For five years she partnered with the Pennsylvania Department of Health and Pennsylvania Department of Corrections to design and implement several statewide health initiatives that are still being used today.

Launching Lives's services encompass both individual and group coaching, live workshops, keynote speeches, teleseminars and webinars, small group facilitation, and retreats. Sylvia also creates products to augment the coaching experience such as an audio program called "Launching Leaders with Sylvia: 5 Essentials for First Time Managers" and a downloadable workbook entitled "Overloaded and Overwhelmed? 10 Strategies for Gaining Control." She also writes a regular feature column for the Sunday edition of the *Harrisburg Patriot News* Business/Money section and a monthly ezine distributed across the country. She has authored over 150 business articles that are pub-

---

lished on the internet and three special reports for persons in management positions.

She is an active member of the Harrisburg Regional Chamber of Commerce and the West Shore Chamber of Commerce, serving on various committees for each, and she is a member of Executive Women International, The National Association of Female Executives, Human Resources Professionals of Central Pennsylvania, the Women's Leadership Network affiliated with the United Way of the Capital Region, and Toastmasters International. A 2010 MS Leadership Award recipient and Central Pennsylvania MS Society board member, Sylvia believes strongly in serving her community.

Having successfully navigated several significant personal tragedies and challenges in her life, Sylvia brings great life experience and empathy to both her coaching and speaking engagements.

www.ingramcontent.com/pod-product-compliance
Lightning Source LLC
Chambersburg PA
CBHW070522200326
41519CB00013B/2898